Cambridge El

MW00635560

Elements in Cognitive Linguistics
edited by
Sarah Duffy
Northumbria University
Nick Riches
Newcastle University

COGNITIVE LINGUISTICS AND LANGUAGE EVOLUTION

Michael Pleyer
Nicolaus Copernicus University in Toruń
Stefan Hartmann
Heinrich Heine University Düsseldorf

CAMBRIDGE
UNIVERSITY PRESS

Shaftesbury Road, Cambridge CB2 8EA, United Kingdom

One Liberty Plaza, 20th Floor, New York, NY 10006, USA

477 Williamstown Road, Port Melbourne, VIC 3207, Australia

314–321, 3rd Floor, Plot 3, Splendor Forum, Jasola District Centre,
New Delhi – 110025, India

103 Penang Road, #05–06/07, Visioncrest Commercial, Singapore 238467

Cambridge University Press is part of Cambridge University Press & Assessment,
a department of the University of Cambridge.

We share the University's mission to contribute to society through the pursuit of
education, learning and research at the highest international levels of excellence.

www.cambridge.org
Information on this title: www.cambridge.org/9781009476065

DOI: 10.1017/9781009385022

© Michael Pleyer and Stefan Hartmann 2024

First published 2024

A catalogue record for this publication is available from the British Library.

ISBN 978-1-009-47606-5 Hardback
ISBN 978-1-009-38498-8 Paperback
ISSN 2633-3325 (online)
ISSN 2633-3317 (print)

Cognitive Linguistics and Language Evolution

Elements in Cognitive Linguistics

DOI: 10.1017/9781009385022
First published online: March 2024

Michael Pleyer
Nicolaus Copernicus University in Toruń

Stefan Hartmann
Heinrich Heine University Düsseldorf

Author for correspondence: Michael Pleyer, pleyer@umk.pl

Abstract: The evolution of language has developed into a large research field. Two questions are particularly relevant for this strand of research. Firstly, how did the human capacity for language emerge? Secondly, which processes of cultural evolution are involved both in the evolution of human language from non-linguistic communication and in the continued evolution of human languages? Much research on language evolution that addresses these two questions is highly compatible with the usage-based approach to language pursued in cognitive linguistics. Focusing on key topics such as comparing human language and animal communication, experimental approaches to language evolution, and evolutionary dynamics in language, this Element gives an overview of the current state-of-the-art of language evolution research and discusses how cognitive linguistics and research on the evolution of language can cross-fertilise each other. This title is also available as Open Access on Cambridge Core.

Keywords: cognitive linguistics, usage-based approaches, language evolution, animal communication, cultural evolution

ISBNs: 9781009476065 (HB), 9781009384988 (PB), 9781009385022 (OC)
ISSNs: 2633-3325 (online), 2633-3317 (print)

Contents

1 Introduction

The question of how language evolved is probably as old as the scientific study of language itself, and it continues to stir controversial debates that often relate to the very nature of language. Any account of the evolution of language has to answer the question of what it actually is that evolved: is it an innate capacity or a complex configuration of domain-general cognitive skills? Such questions are at the centre of language evolution research, an interdisciplinary field that has been enjoying growing popularity since the 1990s. In this Element, we offer a brief review of pertinent research on language evolution from the perspective of cognitive linguistics, and we discuss what a cognitive-linguistic perspective can add to the study of language evolution. In doing so, we follow up on previous work, including our own, that has argued that cognitive linguistics, and particularly Construction Grammar as arguably the most influential approach under the broad umbrella of 'cognitive linguistics', provides a suitable framework for studying the evolution of language (e.g., Arbib 2012; Hurford 2012; Pleyer & Winters 2014; Sinha 2017; Pleyer & Hartmann 2020; Verhagen 2021). We will also discuss how findings from language evolution research can, in turn, inform cognitive-linguistic theorising.

Before doing so, we briefly need to define the scope of language evolution research. The term *language evolution* is notoriously ambiguous as it can either refer to the evolutionary emergence of language or to the continued development of fully fledged human language(s) (Tamariz & Kirby 2016). Haspelmath (2016) has criticised such a conflation of 'origins of language' on the one hand and 'language change' on the other. But as Mendívil-Giró (2019: 24) points out, such an apparent conflation follows naturally from an approach that conceives of languages as social and cultural objects (as does cognitive linguistics). According to such an approach, 'there is every reason to suppose that the very first grammatical constructions emerged in the same way as those observed in more recent history' (Bybee 2010: 202). Domain-general cognitive, social, and interactional processes are the basis of the emergence of linguistic structure both in language change and language evolution (also see Ibbotson 2020: 16). As such, we argue that the scope of language evolution research encompasses both the origins of language and the processes that lead from very early forms of language, often captured in terms of a hypothesised protolanguage (Tallerman 2012), to fully fledged human language. Consequently, we will cover both aspects in this Element.

The relationship between cognitive linguistics and language evolution is a bilateral one. On the one hand, language evolution research is highly relevant to our understanding of language when we take the 'cognitive commitment'

(Lakoff 1990) of cognitive linguistics seriously. According to the cognitive commitment, analyses and theories in cognitive linguistics need to take into account what is known about cognition from other disciplines (cf. Evans & Green 2006). This means that cognitive linguistics also needs to be informed by what is known about the cognitive underpinnings of language in language evolution research. Such an approach also goes hand in hand with a 'commitment to look for converging evidence', that is, a commitment to actively seek out evidence from other disciplines on the role of explanatory cognitive factors used in cognitive linguistics (Evans & Green 2006). In his call for a 'cognitive evolutionary linguistics', Verhagen (2021: 11) re-conceptualises these commitments in terms of a 'biological commitment'. It specifies more precisely what is already implicit in these commitments, namely that what we say about communicative behaviour 'should also be compatible with what we know about communication in organisms in general and about cognition in general'.

On the other hand, cognitive linguistics also has a vital role in specifying the cognitive and interactional factors central to human language, whose evolution needs to be explained by any account of language evolution (Győri 2021). This is expressed in Jackendoff's (2010) dictum, 'Your theory of language evolution depends on your theory of language'. For example, a usage-based view of language sees knowledge of language as represented in a learned network of constructions of differing degrees of schematicity and complexity, which is mutually shared to the degree that it enables interlocutors to co-create contextually scaffolded meaning in interaction. From an evolutionary perspective, the question then becomes how the cognitive abilities, as well as the social structures supporting them, evolved (Pleyer & Hartmann 2020).

In Section 2, we will take a closer comparative look at human language and other animal communication systems. Much previous research comparing human language and animal communication has claimed that there is a 'qualitative' difference between the two (e.g., Bickerton 1990; Berwick & Chomsky 2016). However, more recent work has shown that many animal communication systems are much more complex than previously thought. Overall, this research indicates that there is much more continuity between human language and animal communication systems in terms of the different structuring mechanisms giving rise to communicative structures as well as regarding the importance of pragmatics, context, and social learning (e.g., Engesser & Townsend 2019; Pleyer & Hartmann 2020; Hobaiter et al. 2022).

Section 3 discusses what we can learn from decades of research on language-trained animals (e.g., Lyn 2012). Here, we will focus again on cognitive similarities (e.g., the ability to learn symbolic associations and basic pragmatic and structural sensitivity) and differences. Similar to our discussion of animal communication, these differences are seen more as a matter of degree, not of kind (e.g., differences in the size of storage of associations, the schematicity, and abstractness of such stored associations, and differences in pragmatic and contextual influence on interpretation).

Section 4 will introduce the influential hypothesis that language builds on joint attention, cooperation, and shared intentionality (e.g., Tomasello 2008, 2014). Here, we will focus on the fact that many other animals have highly sophisticated social cognition (e.g., Seyfarth & Cheney 2015; Bettle & Rosati 2021). For instance, many non-human animals can understand others' goals and attention and show some degree of perspective-taking and cooperation. However, there seem to be differences in that human communication is characterised by a much higher degree of cooperativeness, perspective-taking, and the negotiation and awareness of shared goals and the use of pragmatic inferences (e.g., Tomasello 2017).

Section 5 gives an overview of how hypotheses about language evolution have been tested experimentally, mainly focusing on behavioural studies with human participants but also taking computational modelling work into account. We focus on two influential paradigms that have been used extensively in research on human symbolic evolution in general and on language evolution in particular: experimental semiotics is an approach in which participants are required to communicate without language, which often entails that they are required to ground novel communication systems in interaction. In iterated learning (IL), on the other hand, participants are trained on an artificial language that is then transmitted from participant to participant, thus simulating the historical chain of transmission characteristic not only of language but virtually all kinds of cultural artefacts. The two paradigms have been combined in many ways and given rise to complex experimental set-ups that combine learning, communication, and transmission, thus investigating a wide variety of system-internal as well as social and environmental factors that influence linguistic structure.

In Section 6, we turn to the real-world dynamics of language, focusing on two complementary domains: on the one hand, we discuss the implications of historical language change for understanding language evolution. On the other hand, we discuss what we can learn from developing sign languages. The so-called 'emergent' sign languages such as Nicaraguan Sign Language (NSL) and Al-Sayyid Bedouin Sign Language have often been cited as paragon examples of the evolution of a new language. However, some of the guiding assumptions in this line of research have recently been questioned, especially as they tend to exoticise the languages in question as well as their users, which in turn has implications for our understanding of these languages as 'special' cases of language evolution.

We conclude with a brief discussion of the relationship between cognitive linguistics and language evolution, arguing that the usage-based perspective of cognitive linguistics and the current mainstream view of language evolution as a process of cultural evolution are highly compatible.

2 Comparing the 'Design Features' of Language and Animal Communication

This section adopts a comparative perspective on human language. We will compare human language with animal cognition and communication and ask to what degree there are similarities and differences in the underlying cognitive and interactional processes and mechanisms.

Reflecting the general approach of this Element, the aims of this section are again twofold: on the one hand, we will ask what can be learned about human language by comparing it to other animal communication systems. Specifically, we will look at the implications of current research on animal communication for cognitive linguistics. That is, to what degree are cognitive-linguistic conceptualisations of language, and its cognitive and interactional underpinnings, compatible and convergent with research on animal communication and cognition? And to what degree can such research contribute to theory-building in cognitive linguistics? This reflects the cognitive commitment and the commitment to seeking converging evidence (see Section 1).

On the other hand, the aim is to take an explicitly cognitive-linguistic perspective on animal communication and cognition as well as the implications of research on animal communication and cognition on theories of language evolution. That is, what can cognitive linguistics contribute to the study of animal communication and cognition? In some way, this also reflects another commitment of cognitive linguistics, the 'generalisation commitment' (Lakoff 1990; Evans & Green 2006). According to this commitment, cognitive linguistics seeks to explain language in terms of general cognitive principles. From a cognitive-linguistic view, we can therefore try to generalise beyond humans and ask whether particular cognitive principles operate in human language as well as animal communication. Here, the question then becomes whether explanatory cognitive principles and capacities proposed in cognitive linguistics can also be applied to analyse properties of animal communication. In turn, this also means that if a particular cognitive ability used to explain aspects of language in cognitive linguistics is not found to the same degree in other animals, this has direct implications for theories of language evolution. Specifically, cognitive linguistics might stress the importance of particular cognitive and interactional mechanisms, which then might be found to be expressed more strongly in humans or even to be absent in other animals. This then would represent an 'evolutionary target' of processes and properties that must have evolved in the human lineage to make linguistic interaction possible. In other words, this can give potential insights into 'what is special about human language'.[1] Such a cognitive-linguistic view can help elucidate which cognitive and social prerequisites had to be in place for human language to evolve. Based on this, a comparative perspective can shed light on how the social and communicative behaviour of non-human animals compares to these prerequisites.

So far, detailed engagements with animal communication have been relatively limited, although it is increasingly gaining more attention. For example, in previous work, we have investigated the implications of animal communication for language evolution from a usage-based perspective (Pleyer & Hartmann 2020), reviewing how recent findings in animal communication can make contact with usage-based and constructionist approaches. Further, we have argued that applying concepts from usage-based and constructionist approaches can offer new perspectives for analysing human language and animal communication in a shared framework. Christiansen and Chater (2022) also compare human language and animal communication from a broadly usage-based perspective. They argue that in contrast to animal communication, meaning in linguistic interaction is co-created in interaction and instantiated online. It is characterised by improvisation, creativity, and the cultural transmission of previously successful bouts of the co-creating of meaning in interaction. Amphaeris et al. (2021) argue that critical cognitive processes demonstrated by cognitive linguistics to be foundational for language, such as social cognition and symbolic cognition, can be found in animal cognition to differing degrees. In their view, this supports the theory that language evolved on the basis of animal cognition. Lastly, Amphaeris et al. (2022) propose to capture the relationship between human language and animal communication in terms of prototype theory. They explicitly contrast this proposal to an all-or-nothing view of a feature of human language being present in animal communication or not, as well as to a view that sees animal communication and human language as lying on a continuous spectrum. Instead, they advocate a prototype-based

---

[1] Talking about language being 'special' is often tied to 'human exceptionalism'. This in turn is often interpreted as a value judgement of 'human superiority'. However, it is important to note that the notion of 'progress' has no place in evolution. Animals are adapted to particular niches, and should be analysed with relation to the niches they are adapted to, not with regard to teleological value judgements of 'more and less advanced' species. Each species is special in the way it is adapted to a particular niche. For example, bats are special in using echolocation, and elephants are special in having a long prehensile trunk. In evolutionary biology, a trait that distinguishes a particular taxon (such as species, like humans from chimpanzees, or genera, such as 'pan' from 'Homo') is called an 'autapomorphy' (Suddendorf 2008). Language, on this view, is just one particular autapomorphy that distinguishes our species.

view in which phenomena are categorised in terms of family resemblances, graded typicality, as well as overlaps (see also Wacewicz et al. 2020).

2.1 Hockett's 'Design Features' Approach

Animal communication and its similarities and differences with human language have been the focus of intense debate for a long time (e.g., Radick 2007; see also references in Krause 2017). Animal communication has been discussed from the perspective of philosophy (e.g., Stegmann 2013), biology (e.g., Hauser 1996; Smith & Harper 2003; Bradbury & Vehrencamp 2011), primatology (e.g., Seyfarth & Cheney 2010), comparative psychology (e.g., Tomasello 2008), and of course linguistics (e.g., Anderson 2004; Hurford 2007, 2012). Within linguistics, the most influential approach has been Hockett's proposal of 'design features' (Hockett 1959, 1960, 1963).

In particular, Hockett proposed several 'design features' characterising human language whose presence or absence in other animal communication systems can be investigated comparatively (see Table 1). His initial list (Hockett 1959) features seven such features, which in Hockett (1960) were extended to thirteen, and in Hockett (1963) extended again to sixteen. These design features are still extremely popular in linguistics, and it is the classification of communication systems most frequently used in introductory linguistics textbooks (Wacewicz et al. 2023a). However, the design feature approach has not been without (sometimes intense) criticism (e.g., Oller & Griebel 2004; Wacewicz & Żywiczyński 2015), and several researchers have adapted and updated Hockett's proposals for their own 'design feature' lists (Aitchison 2008; O'Grady et al. 2017; Johansson 2021).

On the one hand, criticisms revolve around features that should *not* be included in the list. For example, Johansson (2021) rightly points out that the first five of Hockett's design features (vocal-auditory channel, broadcast transmission and directional reception, rapid fading, and complete feedback) take spoken language as the default and do not apply to other forms of human language. For instance, sign languages do not make use of the vocal-auditory channel but instead make use of the visual modality. Here, it can be argued that Hockett's (1960) design features reflect the ableist ideology of orality at the time in which sign languages were not recognised as full languages, which only slowly began to change with the work of Stokoe (2005) and others (see McBurney 2001 for discussion).[2]

---

[2] It has to be noted that at least Hockett and Altmann (1968) sometimes are explicit in stating that these design features are 'shared by all human spoken languages' (Hockett & Altmann 1968) or refer to a property being a design feature of 'human speech' (Hockett & Altmann 1968). However, Hockett also often fails to make this distinction, stating that these design features 'are found in every language on which we have reliable information' (Hockett 1963) and explicitly calling them 'design-features of language' (Hockett 1960).

Table 1 Hockett's design features (Hockett 1960, 1963; Hockett & Altmann 1968) with an explanation of the feature, comments, and critique of a feature, and estimates of the potential presence of features in other animals based on current evidence.

Design feature	Explanation	Comment	Presence in other animals
Vocal-auditory channel	Spoken language functions via the emission and reception of sound waves	Does not apply to all human languages, for example, signed languages or written language	Characteristic of all vocal-auditory communication systems
Broadcast transmission and directional reception	All receivers within range can perceive the signal and the sound source can be localised	Does not apply to all human languages, for example, signed languages (which require a 'line of sight' between signaller and receiver) or written language. Direct consequence of communication in the vocal-auditory channel	Characteristic of all vocal-auditory communication systems
Rapid fading (transitoriness)	The sound of speech fades rapidly; it does not hover in the air	Does not apply to all human languages, for example, written language. Although the bodily properties of sign language communication also do not remain permanently available, it can be debated whether they fall under 'rapid fading' to the same degree as sound waves. Direct consequence of communication in the vocal-auditory channel	Characteristic of all vocal-auditory communication systems

Table 1 (cont.)

Design feature	Explanation	Comment	Presence in other animals
Interchangeability	Adult members of a speech community can be both producers and receivers of signals interchangeably	Might not universally apply, for example, in written language. For instance, it might be possible that someone can read Chinese characters without being able to write the characters themselves by hand. Another example is receptive or passive bilingualism, in which an individual can understand a language but does not produce it themselves (Sherkina-Lieber 2020)	Present in many vocal-auditory communication systems. However, in many other animals, specific calls are only emitted by males, or only by females, respectively, for example in monkeys (Stephan & Zuberbühler 2016) or songbirds in northern temperate climate zones (Searcy & Andersson 1986; Riebel et al. 2019)
Complete/total feedback	Speakers can perceive their own output, thereby receiving immediate feedback on their own production		Potentially present in all vocal-auditory communication systems
Specialisation	Signals are 'specialised' for communication. They are not cues, that is, by-products of some other functional behaviour. The system is designed 'to trigger' a response in the recipient	Does not consider the question of intentionality in animal communication (Townsend et al. 2017)	Many other animals use signals, including bees, monkeys, apes, many other mammals, and birds (Bradbury & Vehrenkamp 2011; Freeberg et al. 2021)

Semanticity	Linguistic signals have meaning and can be used referentially	The nature of the 'meaning' and cognitive representation of the content of animal signals is difficult to untangle. There might be different degrees of semanticity. Focus on semanticity underplays the importance of pragmatic processes of contextual interpretation (see Section 2.2.1)	Functionally referential communication is widespread, for example, in alarm calls (e.g., Scarantino & Clay 2015). Evidence for extraction of information from calls, for example, in chimpanzees (Crockford et al. 2017), Diana monkeys (Zuberbühler et al. 1999), and Japanese tits (Suzuki 2018)
Arbitrariness	There is no relationship between form of a word and its meaning	Arbitrariness as a linguistic term might not be easily applicable to animal communication (Watson et al. 2022). A focus on arbitrariness leads to an underestimation of the role of iconicity, systematicity, and motivation in language (Dingemanse et al. 2015a; Pleyer et al. 2017)	Present in many other animals such as chimpanzees and other non-human primates, bees, and songbirds (Townsend et al. 2022)

Table 1 (cont.)

Design feature	Explanation	Comment	Presence in other animals
Discreteness	Linguistic signals constitute a discrete repertoire, not a continuous one. They consist of basic signalling units such as phonemes and words	The cognitive foundations of discreteness need to be taken into account, for example categorical perception, whereby even continuous signals are interpreted categorically (Zhang et al. 2023a)	A number of animals seem to represent signals as discrete categories and possess repertoires of discrete signals, including zebra finches and other songbirds (Wiley 2018; Zhang et al. 2023b)
Displacement	We can talk about things that aren't present in the communicative situation but are remote in time and/or place	Displacement is a matter of degree, not an absolute term. Displacement in human language is a result of semanticity and openness/productivity	Limited displacement in bees (von Frisch 1967) and Cambell's monkeys (Zuberbühler 2002). Great apes are capable of pointing communicatively to absent and displaced objects (Lyn et al. 2014; Bohn et al. 2015)
Openness/productivity	Human language can express new messages that have never been produced before	Seems to depend on duality of patterning and semanticity (Wiley 2018). Existing constructions can be assigned new meanings, as in polysemy, metonymy, metaphor, idioms, and so on (Hockett 1963)	Bees can potentially refer to locations that have never been referred to before, but they cannot assign new meanings to existing signals (Hockett 1963). Other than that, other animals seem to be limited in the meanings they can express

Cultural transmission/ tradition	Linguistic conventions are transmitted and change from generation to generation	Cultural transmission in humans is not limited to language. Culturally transmitted behaviours of all kinds are characteristic of cumulative culture (Tomasello 1999; Tomasello et al. 2005)	Bees show evidence of cultural transmission (Jiang et al. 2018), as does bird song (Catchpole & Slater 2008). In chimpanzees, different forms of the 'grooming handclasp' seem to be culturally transmitted (Leeuwen & Hoppitt 2023). Cultural transmission of non-communicative behaviours is widespread in animals (Whiten 2019) (see Section 2.2.2)
Duality of patterning	Meaningless units (phonemes, /p/, /e/, /n/) can be combined into meaningful units (words, *pen*), which in turn can be combined to form bigger meaningful units (phrases and utterances)	Phonological combinatoriality and meaning-based grammatical compositionality should be distinguished, also in terms of the cognitive processes employed and the evolutionary challenges in evolving these features (Zuidema & De Boer 2018)	The calls of chestnut-crowned babblers are composed of meaningless shared building blocks (Engesser et al. 2019). Limited compositionality can be found in a number of species, such as chimpanzees (Leroux et al. 2023), Campbell's monkeys and southern pied babblers (Townsend et al. 2018), and Japanese tits (Suzuki et al. 2016)

Table 1 (cont.)

Design feature	Explanation	Comment	Presence in other animals
Prevarication	We can lie or say things that are meaningless	Based on the design features of semanticity, displacement, and openness/productivity	Probably not, but several animals show deception in communication (Flower 2022)
Reflexiveness	Using language, we can communicate about the system of language on a meta-level	Based on the design features of semanticity and openness/productivity	Probably not
Learnability	Languages are learned	Based on the design feature of cultural transmission/tradition	Evidence of usage learning in a number of animals, but more limited evidence of production learning. At least some great ape gestures are probably learned (Cartmill & Hobaiter 2019). Social learning of behaviour can be found in numerous species (Whiten 2019) (see Section 2.2.2)

On the other hand, criticisms focus on missing features that should be added to the list or replace an existing feature. For example, Johansson (2021) proposes *intentional production* as an additional feature, which is also echoed in Aitchison's (2008) proposal to add *spontaneous usage*. Aitchison (2008) also adds other elements to her design feature list: *turn-taking, structure-dependence*, and the *ability to read intentions*. Watson et al. (2022) argue that the notion of 'arbitrariness' is such an intrinsically linguistic concept that it is difficult to apply it to animal communication. They therefore propose to replace it with 'optionality' as the central underpinning of linguistic arbitrariness. Optionality refers to the ability to associate one signal form with different communicative functions, or different communicative functions being expressed by the same signal form. As they show, a concept such as optionality can be readily demonstrated in a number of animal communication systems. For example, in great ape gestures, the same gesture can be used for multiple communicative functions (Byrne et al. 2017; Hobaiter et al. 2022; see Section 2.2.1). The concept of optionality, in turn, can be decomposed into sub-aspects, which allows for an even more fine-grained comparison of human language and other animal communication systems.

These additions and replacements, which relate to cognitive and social aspects of language, point to a different problem with the 'design feature' list, namely that Hockett's original formulation does not address the cognitive and interactional dimension of language and does not characterise appropriately more foundational and defining properties of language as a system, instead focusing on superficial and at times epiphenomenal aspects (Oller 2004; Johansson 2021). In fact, Wacewicz and Żywiczyński (2015) have gone so far as to argue that Hockett's design feature approach is a 'non-starter' and not a helpful framework for comparing human language and animal communication and investigating the evolution of language. The problem in their view is that Hockett's design features approach does not treat language as 'a suite of sensorimotor, cognitive and social abilities that enable the use but also acquisition of language by biological creatures' (Wacewicz & Żywiczyński 2015; see also Pleyer & Zhang 2022). This critique is especially relevant from a cognitive-linguistic point of view.

Another problem, which again is particularly salient from a cognitive-linguistic perspective (see also Amphaeris et al. 2022), was, in fact, already formulated by Hockett himself (Hockett & Altmann 1968): '[E]ach feature seems to be set forth in an all-or-none manner, although upon closer scrutiny some of them are surely matters of degree'.

Lastly, Hockett's design feature list has been criticised for being precisely that, a list. That is, it didn't account for how features might be related to each other and how they can be integrated into a broader context (Oller & Griebel 2004; see also Wacewicz & Żywiczyński 2015).

In fact, Hockett & Altmann (1968) propose that the different design features of Hockett (1963) can be generalised into four frameworks of inquiry regarding communicative behaviour, which relate to: (a) the channel(s) of communication, (b) the social setting, (c) 'Features related to the behavioural antecedents and consequences of communicative acts', and (d) the interplay of environment, social settings, and biology in the change and continuity of communication systems. These four frameworks are then further specified in terms of sub-aspects and questions about the framework leading to a total of twenty-four questions to guide inquiries about animal communicative behaviour. However, this revision of the 'design features' seems to have largely been ignored and has not fuelled descriptions of communication systems in a meaningful way.

While still acknowledging the importance of Hockett's pioneering work, Oller & Griebel (2004: 4) summarise: 'Ultimately, it has become clear that many of the features formulated by Hockett were simply ill-defined, yielding unnecessary and confusing overlap among features, lack of clarity regarding boundaries implied by the definitions, and a failure to account for hierarchical relationships among features'.

This contrasts with the noted continuing popularity of Hockett's design feature approach in linguistics and linguistics textbooks. However, both textbooks and researchers referring to Hockett's design features mostly only list selected properties from Hockett's list, sometimes with direct reference to Hockett and sometimes without (Wacewicz et al. 2023a). The most frequently mentioned features characterising human language are *displacement, arbitrariness, cultural transmission*, and *productivity/openness/creativity*. Here we also see the problematic interconnection of design features, as displacement is a natural consequence of open-ended semantics. Surely, these properties, as well as properties such as *learnability, semanticity*, and *duality of patterning*, are essential aspects of human language. They are also potentially useful for comparison with animal communication systems if it is acknowledged that we should treat them not as boxes to be ticked or not. Instead, they should be seen as properties that we need to analyse in their ecological, cognitive, behavioural, social, and structural dimensions with an additional view towards their relations among each other (Wacewicz & Żywiczyński 2015; Pleyer & Zhang 2022). But as we have seen, other properties also need to be added.

2.2 Animal Communication Systems and Human Language

In the following, we will illustrate this perspective by looking at two 'design features' in more detail: semanticity and learnability. These discussions will not be exhaustive; as we have seen, many more properties need to be discussed.[3] But in line with Amphaeris et al. (2022), this discussion should be seen more as establishing some core prototypical features of language with graded properties. However, they will illustrate possible ways to compare human language and animal communication from a cognitive perspective. That is, we will adopt an explicitly cognitive-linguistic view of human language and its relation to cognition and interaction. As we will discuss these properties in contact and in an active dialogue with recent research on animal communication, it is also possible that it needs to be revised depending on the evidence and its analysis. Overall, what should become clear from this is that we should not look for dichotomous 'all-or-nothing' differences but instead ask to what degree mechanisms found in human language are similar or different to those found in other animal communication systems (Engesser & Townsend 2019; Pleyer & Hartmann 2020; Amphaeris et al. 2022; Pleyer et al. 2022).

2.2.1 Semanticity

When discussing semanticity in animal communication and human language from a cognitive-linguistic perspective, we have to note that cognitive linguistics does not see semantics as an isolated domain. Cognitive linguistics generally rejects the strict distinction between semantics and pragmatics. Linguistic meaning is intricately tied not only to encyclopaedic world knowledge and contextual factors (see, e.g., Langacker 2008: 39). It is also interactional (see, e.g., Langacker 2008: 42). That means it is actively constructed and co-created in interactive contexts. Linguistic utterances are seen as prompts for the dynamic construction of meaning in interaction, making use of various cognitive, sociocognitive, contextual, and interactive dimensions (e.g., Fauconnier 2004; Evans & Green 2006). Constructions and utterances, therefore, also do not have fixed meanings but have 'meaning potentials' tied to contexts of use that are always interpreted and influenced by the pragmatics of the interaction (Geeraerts 2006; see also Sperber & Wilson 1995). Consequently, cognitive linguistics also emphasises the dynamicity of linguistic meaning: concepts like metaphor and metonymy (Lakoff & Johnson 1980) as well as conceptual blending (Fauconnier & Turner 2002) have been used to systematise the flexible ways in which language users exploit the meaning potential of linguistic expressions. For example, metaphor selectively seizes aspects of an expression's meaning and maps them to another,

---

[3] For instance, we do not discuss one of the most hotly contested topics in animal communication here, that of 'animal syntax' and whether compositionality can be found in non-human communication. A usage-based perspective on this topic is presented by Pleyer et al. (2022).

usually abstract domain (e.g., TIME IS SPACE: *We moved the meeting forward*). Conceptual blending refers to a hypothesised domain-general process that allows us to 'blend' aspects of various mental spaces in complex integration networks – for example, individuals at various stages of their lives in a sentence like *When I was your age, Taylor Swift wasn't even born*. Cognitive linguists have also emphasised the role of domain-general capacities like categorisation (see, e.g., Lakoff 1987) underlying the construction of meaning. Cognitive approaches to semantics are strongly influenced by prototype theory, according to which membership to a category is not an all-or-nothing affair but a graded phenomenon (see, e.g., Rosch 1978; Taylor 2003). For instance, a concept like *bachelor* can clearly be applied to a twenty-year-old man who is not in a relationship, while it is at least debatable whether it applies to the pope (Lakoff 1987: 70). The dynamicity of linguistic meaning is also captured by the concept of *construal* that plays a key role in many cognitive-linguistic approaches, with Hoffmann (2022: 286) defining it as a 'mental perspective on a scene that finds its expression in linguistic utterances'. Language, on this view, then, is fundamentally perspectival. Language users possess a repertoire of constructions that enables them to construe situations and events in different ways and organise conceptual content from different points of view (e.g., Verhagen 2007; Langacker 2008). This holds both for instances of grammatical and lexical construal. For example, the same situation can be described by different utterances such as *I gave her my favourite book*, *I gave my favourite book away*, *She received a book*, *A person received something*, and so on, thereby distributing attention and salience to different aspects of the situation and construing it from different perspectives. Lexical choices also present different construals, reflecting and prompting conceptualisations that highlight different aspects of an entity or situation. For example, a speaker of English can choose which elements to bring into focus through the use of verbs such as *cost, charge, spend, pay, sell*, and *buy* (such as *She bought a PS5, The vendor charged her £ 539 for the PS5, She paid £ 539 for the PS5*, etc.). They all call upon the 'commercial event' frame, but they focus attention and make salient different elements and relations of the frame. Similarly, in the domain of lexical choice, the same entity can be called, for example, an *animal*, a *mammal*, a *dog*, a *border collie*, *Rico*, or *our little genius*. This means that the same event can be described differently, highlighting different elements and participants (Radden & Dirven 2007). This, then, is the particular perspective that cognitive linguistics and usage-based approaches bring to questions about the semanticity of animal communication.

There are two famous examples in discussions of communicative signals providing information about a referent: the 'dance language' of honeybees (von Frisch 1967) and the alarm calls of vervet monkeys (Cheney & Seyfarth 1990).

Honeybees perform a complex geometrical 'dance' that communicates a flower's location and quality (Hurford 2012). Vervet monkeys were shown to emit three different alarm calls for 'snakes', 'leopards', and 'eagles'.

The honeybee dance also clearly seems to indicate the design feature of 'displacement' because bees provide information about an absent referent. But here, we also see a problem with the term displacement because bees provide information about an absent entity. However, what they can communicate about the referent is extremely limited, namely its location and quality. This means this system does not exhibit the design features of *openness* or *productivity* (Hockett 1963). Therefore, one proposal to make the notion of displacement in human language more productive is that, first, it should be specified what kind of displacement we are talking about and also try to tie it to possible cognitive correlates. For example, the capacity to conceptualise absent entities, as well as situations in the past and future, is linked to capacities for episodic memory (Tulving 2001) and mental time travel (Suddendorf & Corballis 2007; cf. Pleyer & Zhang 2022).

This also brings us to the problem of assessing mental representations in other animals. This is, of course especially prevalent for a species whose brain measures about 0.4–0.6 mm^3 and has about 1 million neurons (compared to ~1400cc and 86 billion neurons in humans; Azevedo et al. 2009; Menzel 2012). But it is just as much a problem for other animals, as we do not have access to their mental representations (we cannot ask them) but have to make inferences from various sources, such as their behaviour.

This problem has also been the topic of intense discussion when investigating vervet monkey alarm calls (Price et al. 2015; Vonk 2020) and many other species that produce such calls (see Townsend & Manser 2013; Gill & Bierema 2013 for reviews). As vervet monkeys show appropriate behavioural responses specific to the call (e.g., by standing up and looking around on hearing the 'snake' alarm call), one proposal has been that this can be captured in terms of 'functional reference' (see Macedonia & Evans 1993; Wheeler & Fischer 2012; Scarantino & Clay 2015 for discussion). As such, there has been the proposal that in this context, these calls can be seen as 'word-like' as they couple arbitrary sounds with external phenomena and potentially offer a link between animal communication and linguistic semantics (Bickerton 2009). From a cognitive-linguistic perspective, we could, therefore, ask whether they are some kind of 'protoconstructions' representing form–meaning pairings. However, several studies have started to concentrate instead on the perspective of the receiver and their interpretation of these calls, often from a cognitive perspective (e.g., Hurford 2007). Specifically, these questions revolve around topics such as asking (a) whether other animals form any kind of (conceptual) representations upon hearing a call and (b) how contextual information is used by recipients to interpret the call. Regarding the first question, a snake-specific alarm call seems to evoke a visual search image for snake-like objects in Japanese tits (Suzuki 2018). Diana monkeys seem to retain an expectation of seeing predators after hearing alarm calls (Zuberbühler et al. 1999). So, there is some evidence that animals form at least some kind of stored association between a call and a referent. However, the role of context in call interpretation has received increasing attention because many call types seem not to be limited to one context but instead are produced in multiple contexts (Price et al. 2015).

In a recent study on vervet monkeys, Deshpande et al. (2023) have shown that the famous vervet monkeys, for example, seem to take context into account when hearing alarm calls. Specifically, the vervet monkey male alarm bark, which is often described as a 'leopard' or 'terrestrial predator' alarm call, is also emitted in aggressive intergroup encounters. In playback experiments, Deshpande et al. (2023) showed that vervets looked at the location of the speaker for less time, didn't show a startle response, and were less vigilant compared to when they heard the same call in a non-group encounter situation. The longer-looking time in non-group encounter situations was interpreted as indicating an attempt to gather additional information. As summarised by Seyfarth and Cheney (2010), 'animals' comprehension of vocalisations, as measured by their responses, are highly flexible, modifiable as a result of experience, and show the most parallels with human language'.

The importance of pragmatics and contextual factors is also evident in the gestural domain, particularly in great ape gestures. Great apes show intentional use of gestures, with many repertoires being about seventy to eighty gestures (Byrne et al. 2017). However, just as with the examples of alarm calls just discussed, these gestures can, in a sense, be described as 'polysemous' (Moore 2014; cf. Pleyer 2017), as they 'are all characterized by the use of several different gestures in a single context and the use of a single gesture in multiple contexts' (Liebal et al. 2014: 155). Great ape gestural communication, then, is hugely reliant on pragmatics (Genty & Zuberbühler 2015).

Interestingly, and especially relevant from a usage-based and cognitive-linguistic perspective, this flexible and polysemous meaning of gestures and its dependence on the pragmatics of usage contexts bring this kind of communication much closer to the way that linguistic constructions work in interaction (Pleyer & Hartmann 2020): both linguistic constructions and great ape gestures are used intentionally, are used flexibly in multiple contexts, have their meanings affected by contexts, and are also used in interactive back-and-forth exchanges between individuals (Hobaiter et al. 2022). This also suggests that these properties characterise the evolutionary platform on which human language is built, although human linguistic interaction is made much more powerful by human complex social cognition and the presence of complex ostension and inference in communication (Heintz & Scott-Phillips 2023; see also Section 4).

2.2.2 Learnability

Human language is learned. Usage-based approaches argue that through social interaction throughout the course of language acquisition, children learn a structured network of form–meaning pairings – constructions – of increasing schematicity and abstractness (Tomasello 2003; Ibbotson 2020). In contrast, non-human primate calls seem to be largely innate, and they seem to have very limited vocal production learning capacities (Fischer 2017). For example, cross-fostered monkeys growing up among other monkey species still produce vocalisations of their own species (Owren et al. 1993). However, non-human primates show evidence of 'usage learning'. They still have to learn when exactly to produce a particular call. Young vervet monkeys, for example, initially produce the 'eagle' alarm call for all birds they see but then incrementally 'zoom in' on the correct usage context of aerial predators (Seyfarth & Cheney 1986). Some limited modification of call structure also seems to be possible. For example, male baboon calls are more similar to calls of males they interacted frequently with when compared to males they interacted with less frequently (Fischer et al. 2020). This also opens up the exciting possibility that processes of entrenchment and precursors of conventionalisation (Schmid 2020; Pleyer 2023) operate in animal communication.

Overall, as is the case for semanticity, the evidence that learning plays a role in comprehending calls is much stronger. For example, monkeys can learn the function of the alarm calls of other species (Zuberbühler 2000). But there is also evidence that the meaning of alarm calls is influenced by context and environment. For example, Campbell's monkeys in two different populations seem to have different associated responses to the same call (Schlenker et al. 2014). In one population in the Tai forest (Ivory Coast), their *krak* call often functions as a leopard alarm call. In contrast, in the other population on Tiwai island (Sierra Leone), it acts as a general alarm call (see also Schlenker et al. 2016). This might be explained by the fact that the populations differ in terms of the predators they are exposed to. Whereas the Tai monkeys are exposed to both ground and aerial predators, the Tiwai monkeys are only exposed to aerial predators. A similar situation is observed in the differences in call meaning between two populations of two closely related species, Verreaux's and Coquerel's sifakas (Fichtel & Kappeler 2011). The two populations live in environments that differ in predation threat. The captive Coquerel's sifaka habitat is dominated by aerial predators, whereas the wild-living Coquerel's sifaka population have a high threat of terrestrial predation.

Interestingly, this is reflected in call meaning. 'Growl' calls in the Coquerel's sifaka population seem to be associated with aerial predators. In the Verreaux's sifaka population, it was associated with terrestrial predator responses. In contrast, the call was instead associated with mild disturbances in two populations of each species without a dominant particular predation threat. Overall, then, there is evidence of social learning of call meanings in non-human primates. This again suggests a shared evolutionary platform for this aspect of the dynamic acquisition of contextually modulated form–meaning pairings in human language.

Social learning also has been shown to be relevant in birds and many other species. A recent study has shown that social signal learning even plays a role in honeybees. The waggle dances of bees without the opportunity to observe other dances before their first own dance were significantly disordered. They showed errors in encoding the flight path angle and distance to get to a location (Dong et al. 2023). This indicates that even in cases where there is significant genetic channelling of communication systems, social learning represents a vital process in making the system 'usage-ready'.

3 Signing Apes and Talking Birds: Language-Trained Animals

We have seen that animals exhibit complex communicative behaviour in the wild. However, certain features found in human language seem not to be present, such as complex compositional constructions and the use of an open-ended inventory of form–meaning pairings to collaboratively co-create meaning in interaction. However, it is possible that animals have more complex cognitive capabilities than those evident in their communicative behaviour in the wild. Given the complex cognition of some animals (e.g., De Waal 2016), especially other primates (e.g., Seed & Tomasello 2010), is it possible that they might be able to grasp (aspects of) human language? This has been one of the most popular as well as controversial questions in animal communication (e.g., Seidenberg & Petitto 1979; Sebeok & Umiker-Sebeok 1980; Anderson 2004). This is also reflected in the popularity of popular press books and media attention that this kind of research received in the past. In addition, it is also evident in the fact that many introductory linguistics textbooks (cf. Wacewicz et al. 2023a) and introductions to language acquisition discuss this research extensively (cf. Pleyer & Hartmann 2020). Interest and active research in 'ape language' research have declined significantly over the years, especially following some highly critical evaluations of these experiments (e.g., Terrace et al. 1979) as well as increasing ethical concerns (e.g., Hu 2014).

Nevertheless, the existing research is still of great interest for language evolution research as a way of probing deeper into animals' communicative and cognitive capacities and comparing the human capacity for language with the abilities of other animals. Yet even after over seventy years of research, the controversy about the analysis and implications of 'animal language studies' is unabated. As Tomasello (2017) summarises, 'The "ape language" studies have come and gone, with wildly divergent claims about what they have shown'. However, at least in some respects, there is relative consensus, which we will discuss in the following. Overall, there are two key questions regarding language-training experiments with great apes: (a) are they able to learn symbols, and (b) are they able to learn aspects of the combinatorial structure of language, that is, syntax? Regarding the first question, many researchers argue that great apes do indeed show evidence of this, whereas the second question is much more contested.

The first systematic attempt at teaching an ape language was by Hayes and Hayes (1951). They tried to raise a female chimpanzee, Viki, as much as a human child as possible with the addition of explicit language teaching, including shaping Viki's lips for sound production. After three years, according to Hayes and Hayes (1951), Viki was able to produce three words: 'cup', 'papa', and 'mama'. However, although Viki produced specific sounds intentionally or at least in response to prompts, it requires interpretation to categorise them as English words. 'Papa' sounded like two consecutive lip smacks, and at least in existing videos, 'cup' was produced with Viki putting her hand in front of her mouth and touching her lips to make the sound.[4] In addition, they note that Viki sometimes confused her three words with each other.

One takeaway researchers took from this study was that chimpanzees are probably not able to produce spoken language due to their vocal tract anatomy. However, recent research has shown the high flexibility of mammalian vocal tracts, and simulations have demonstrated that a non-human primate vocal tract, in principle, can produce speech sounds or, in other words, is 'speech-ready' (Fitch et al. 2016).[5] This means that their inability to produce speech is not due to vocal tract anatomy but instead due to the lack of human-like neural control systems for fine-grained vocal motor control.

---

[4] A short clip of Viki producing these 'words' can be found here: www.youtube.com/watch?v=V7QM97fnypw (Accessed 18 May 2023)

[5] For a – somewhat creepy-sounding – synthesized rendition of what a macaque monkey would sound like saying 'Will you marry me?', see here: www.science.org/doi/suppl/10.1126/sciadv.1600723/suppl_file/audio_s2_monkeywymm.wav (Accessed 18 May 2023)

Nevertheless, these considerations led several researchers to try to teach language to great apes using a different modality. These experiments were much more successful, but how much more successful is a matter of debate (see Lyn 2012 for a review). Premack (1971) tried to teach a chimpanzee, Sarah, a 'visual language'. This 'language' was based on pieces of plastic with different colours, shapes, and sizes, which had different meanings and specific ordering rules. He reported the productive use and comprehension of more than ninety-eight signs after intensive training. Rumbaugh and colleagues (Rumbaugh 1977) tried to teach another chimpanzee, Lana, an artificial visual language called 'Yerkish', whose vocabulary consisted of graphical symbols on a lexigram keyboard, reporting a productive and comprehension vocabulary of more than 123 symbols. Using a similar design but a more complex lexigram keyboard and a different teaching regime, including English language immersion, Savage-Rumbaugh et al. (1983) taught two chimpanzees, Austin and Sherman. They reported a productive use of more than sixty-eight symbols and comprehension of more than sixteen symbols.

Given that great apes show evidence of flexible control of their hands, several studies in the 1960s and 1970s tried to teach several great apes a natural language in the visual modality: American Sign Language (ASL). For chimpanzees Washoe (Gardner & Gardner 1969) as well as Moja, Tatu, and Dar (Fouts & Mills 1998), the productive vocabulary reported in peer-reviewed studies ranged from 119 to 160 signs. Chimpanzee Nim Chimpsky was said to produce around 125 signs (Terrace et al. 1979). Gorilla Koko was reported to produce 85–150 signs. In non-peer-reviewed publications, the orangutan Chantek was reported to produce around 150 signs (Miles 1999). For gorilla Koko, the claim has been made that she could produce over 1,000 signs, although these claims were not reported in peer-reviewed publications (Lyn 2012).

However, here, we have to make a significant caveat that, unfortunately, is often misrepresented in the literature. Very often, we find the statement in the literature that these chimpanzees were taught, or use 'sign language' or 'American Sign Language'. However, ASL is a complex natural human language. But most of the teachers in these experiments were not native signers, and many, if not most of them, were not even fluent signers (Anderson 2004: 276). This means that 'in practice the apes were taught signs borrowed from ASL with English word order, not true ASL' (Kaplan 2016). This is somewhat acknowledged by Patterson, who stated that Koko was taught a modified version of ASL called 'gorilla sign language' (Newman 2013), but to what degree this system should be called a 'sign language' is not clear. However, the fact remains that, as Anderson (2004: 280) puts it, the great apes in these experiments had 'virtually no evidence for the grammatical mechanisms of true ASL'. One Deaf assistant in the Nim Chimpsky study also recollects that the other (hearing) trainers were overly generous in what they recognised as a sign even if they only partially resembled ASL signs (Neisser 1983; cf. Kaplan 2016; though see Stokoe 1978 for a more charitable interpretation). Moreover, Kaplan (2016) points out that for the chimpanzees that were studied, many of the gestures interpreted by the researchers as ASL signs were actually naturally occurring gestures in the wild, such as COME/GIMME and HURRY. The latter is particularly significant as in at least one study (Fouts & Fouts 1989); HURRY comprised 65 per cent of the 206 produced signs interpreted as ASL signs.

These considerations are also of fundamental importance when considering the second question, 'Can an ape create a sentence?' (Terrace et al. 1979), that is, if there are ordering principles in great ape 'sign language' production. At least some research indicates incipient tendencies towards broad semantic ordering principles (serial order) in some subjects. The best evidence for this comes from bonobo Kanzi, 'the star pupil' of ape language research. It is generally agreed upon that Kanzi showed the most sophisticated skills of any language-trained primate (Tomasello 2017). He was not only reported to use more than 256 lexigram signs productively and understand ±179 symbols, but he was also tested on English comprehension, in which he was immersed. Over a six-month period, Savage-Rumbaugh et al. (1993) tested both Kanzi and Alia, a human child aged eighteen to twenty-four months during testing, on their comprehension of requests such as *Can you put some toothpaste on your ball?* and *Carry the rock to the bedroom*. They reported his overall accuracy across different types of requests with different construction properties at 71.5 per cent, compared with Alia's 66.6 per cent of accurate responses. This led them to the conclusion that Kanzi's spoken English comprehension is similar to that of a 2.5-year-old child (cf. Hurford 2012; Lyn 2012). However, as Truswell (2017) points out, Kanzi's performance is not the same across the board. In fact, Truswell shows that 'Kanzi doesn't get NP coordinations' (Hurford 2012: 495). For noun phrase-coordination constructions such as *Give the water and the doggie to Rose* or *Give the lighter and the shoe to Rose*, his accuracy falls to 22.2 per cent. For example, in both cases, Kanzi only gave Rose one of the two items. In contrast, Alia's performance was the same as her baseline (68.4 per cent). Truswell (2017: 410) states this 'suggests a species-specific, construction-specific deficit'. Most researchers, therefore, agree that none of the language-trained apes shows evidence of grammatical structuring or hierarchical structure in production or comprehension (e.g., Hurford 2012; Lyn 2012; Truswell 2017). In Construction Grammar terms, there seems to be a difference in the schematicity and abstractness of stored constructions when comparing humans and language-trained animals (Pleyer & Hartmann 2020).

The question of animal grammatical abilities has also been tested in the paradigm of 'artificial grammar learning', especially with primates and birds (see, e.g., ten Cate 2017; ten Cate & Petkov 2019 for reviews). These studies showed evidence of a basic continuity between animal cognition and human language learning capacities, especially in the domain of statistical learning, and some limited ability to detect regularities and dependencies in structured sequences of stimuli (Petkov & ten Cate 2020). However, the current evidence is seen to be 'insufficient to arrive at firm conclusions concerning the limitations of animal grammatical abilities' (ten Cate 2017). One of the most impressive results so far comes from a study of two rhesus monkeys trained to indicate correct sequences of flashing coloured dots on a hexagonal spatial grid that followed a complex 'mirror grammar' (Jiang et al. 2018). This grammar had the supra-regular pattern of AB|BA and ABC|CBA. Monkeys saw the first half of the grammar on a screen and were trained to complete the sequence following the mirror grammar. For example, a flashing dot would first appear in location 1, then location 2, and then location 5. If they then completed the sequence using the correct grammar, in this case, by first touching location 5, then 2, and 1, they were rewarded with water or juice. They were even able to transfer this grammar to longer sequences with a length of 4 (ABCD|DCBA) and 5 (ABCDE|EDCBA) and to novel geometrical layouts, such as a pyramid, a horizontal line, or two hexagons. These results indicate cognitive capacities in animals that approach the hierarchical cognitive complexity of human language. However, one crucial difference to humans is that these monkeys needed literally tens of thousands of trials to learn this grammar (Fitch 2018; Jiang et al. 2018). To put this into perspective, Jiang et al. (2018) also taught this grammar to human five to six year olds. Not only were they vastly more accurate than the monkeys, they also learned it after five trials. Interestingly, Jiang et al. (2018) suggest that this is due to preschoolers using a different strategy, namely chunking, which in usage-based and cognitive-linguistic approaches has been shown to be central to how language is learned (e.g., Tomasello 2003; Bybee 2010; Ibbotson 2020).

Symbol comprehension and production have also been tested in other symbol-trained animals. For example, border collie Rico was shown to understand about 200 sound-item mappings (Kaminski et al. 2004), and could successfully retrieve toys from another room upon hearing the appropriate label. Border collie Chaser even retrieved 1,022 toys with different labels (Pilley & Reid 2011). Interestingly, both dogs showed evidence of 'fast-mapping' – learning a label after a single exposure – and learning through inferential reasoning by exclusion. This means that upon hearing a novel label, they retrieved the correct toy if it was the only one in the set they hadn't learned a label for, and retained knowledge of that label afterwards. A grey parrot, Alex, learned and produced correct labels for '>50 objects, seven colors, five shapes, quantities to eight, three categories (color, shape, material) and used "no," "come here," "wanna go X," and "want Y" (X,Y being appropriate location or item labels). He combined labels to identify, request, comment on, or refuse>150 items and to alter his environment' (Pepperberg 2012: 297). There are also studies of dolphins indicating that they can learn the referential function of novel symbols and gestures, and even some evidence for comprehension of semantic ordering (Pack 2015).

So what does this research tell us about the human ability to learn and use language, and its evolution? In other words, what can we learn from this about the potential 'evolutionary baseline' that human cognition evolved on top of? Basic symbol learning seems to be relatively widespread in different animals. What is more, animals also seem to be able to learn more abstract relations such as 'same' and 'different' (e.g., Hurford 2007), something that has even been demonstrated in bees (Giurfa 2021; cf. Pleyer et al. 2023). They also have been shown to understand relations between symbols, which according to Deacon (1998) is the key feature of truly symbolic cognition. For example, Chaser was able to learn hypernymic common nouns with one-to-many and many-to-one relations ('frisbee', 'ball', and 'toy'). Specifically, she knew each tested item by its proper-noun name, and also was able to categorise all these items under the category 'toy' and a subset of them (e.g., balls of different sizes and colours) under 'balls'. Overall, the evidence suggests that animals, and especially apes, possess many of the cognitive skills requisite for language, such as statistical and sequential learning, categorisation, some semantic ordering principles, and basic symbol learning (Tomasello 2017).

However, then the question becomes what differences explain humans' capacity for language. For one, as we have seen, there seems to be a difference in humans' ability for hierarchical processing. However, there is also a range of other differences that animal language studies demonstrate. One concerns the size of the repertoire these animals learn. The peer-reviewed reported range of productive vocabularies for language-trained apes was between 68 and more than 256 (Lyn 2012). However, this pales in comparison to the number of constructions that humans know. For example, Brysbaert et al. (2016) estimate that 'an average 20-year-old native speaker of American English knows 42,000 lemmas and 4,200 non-transparent multiword expressions' with around 6,000 lemmas added from twenty to sixty years of age. From a constructionist perspective, which would also count semi-filled, unfilled, and more abstract constructions, this estimate would even be much higher (cf. Pleyer 2017). By twenty-four months, the number of words children know already ranges from 100 to 600 (Fenson et al. 1994), clearly beginning to outnumber even the highest scores claimed for language-trained animals. This point is definitely reached when children enter school, a time by which they know about 14,000 words (Templin 1957). Even the non-peer-reviewed claims of Koko knowing 1,000 signs and Kanzi being able to understand 3,000 words, as well as Chaser's documented 1,002 items, pale in comparison. Humans are therefore exceptional in their ability to learn a network of constructions. The capacity for 'massive storage' of constructions in memory seems to be an important evolutionary development in humans (Hurford 2012; Pleyer & Hartmann 2020). This is of particular interest from a usage-based perspective, in which aspects of human memory play a crucial role in explaining the organisation and acquisition of linguistic know-ledge (e.g., Divjak 2019; Schmid 2016).

However, one other significant difference shown by these studies lies in the social domain. More specifically, many differences between the acquisition of symbols in great apes and humans might stem from the fact that humans have special prosocial motivations and sociocognitive and pragmatic abilities. For example, human linguistic interactions are characterised by their 'Mitteilungsbedürfnis' (Fitch 2010), their desire and motivation to share per-spectives and experiences and co-create meaning in interaction. So whereas humans use declarative gestures and declarative utterances from very early on, the vast majority of the utterances produced by language-trained apes are requests (Tomasello 2008). In addition, the apes did not show much interest in the perspectives and contributions of their communicative partners. This is evidenced in their lack of turn-taking, a feature of communication central to human interaction (Levinson 2016). For example, more than half of Nim Chimpsky's utterances interrupted his teacher, and he would also frequently sign at the same time as the teacher, indicating no awareness of interlocutor turns (Kaplan 2016). We will turn to this special role of cooperation and social cognition in language and language evolution next.

4 Cooperation and Communication: The Joint Attention Hypothesis

Language acquisition in humans is fundamentally social. It rests on infants' and young children's sociocognitive abilities as well as their interactional and social motivations. Humans communicate triadically. Much face-to-face com-munication involves the producer and the recipient attending jointly to a third entity (Tomasello 1999). This capacity for joint attention is foundational for language acquisition. For example, from as early as twelve months onwards, infants use gaze following to learn about objects and events (Flom & Johnson 2011). By eighteen months, infants learn to associate a new word not with the object they are currently interested in but with the object the adult is looking at (Baldwin 1993; Baldwin & Moses 2001). Indeed, the role of joint attention is already evident before the emergence of language in children. For example, twelve-month-olds already point declaratively to share attention and interest, and to 'share their perspective'. Importantly, when an interesting event occurs that infants point to, they are only satisfied if it leads to triadic joint attention, that is, if the experimenter exchanges looks between them and the event, not when the experimenter only attends to the event without acknowledgement (Liszkowski et al. 2004). As we have seen, this declarative communicative behaviour seems fundamentally different from how language-trained great apes communicate.

However, children's use of social cognition in language acquisition goes much further than that. They also start to take interlocutors' intentions and knowledge states into account. For example, twenty-four-month-old children learn a new word for the adult's intended action, not the failed one they actually performed (Tomasello & Barton 1994). At the same age, they also learn that a new word refers to something that is new to the adult but not to them (Akhtar et al. 1996). Again, these foundations are already evident in pre-linguistic infants. By fourteen months, infants understand declarative–cooperative pointing gestures (Behne et al. 2005), and exhibit knowledge of what 'we' have experienced together. For example, if being asked to hand the experimenter a toy the experimenter seems to be excited about, infants at this age hand them the toy that is new to the experimenter but not to the infant (Tomasello & Haberl 2003; Moll et al. 2007). At fourteen to eighteen months, they also show more complex evidence of using context and shared experience to interpret gestures. For example, Liebal et al. (2009) had children play a 'cleaning up' game, in which an adult points at an object and an infant puts it into a box. They then had another adult enter the room and point at an object. Infants did not interpret this pointing gesture egocentrically. They did not put the object into the box but instead handed it to the adult. These kinds of experiments offer evidence for a sociocognitive foundation of language acquisition in humans. As Tomasello et al. (2005: 690) put it:

> Saying that only humans have language is like saying that only humans build skyscrapers, when the fact is that only humans (among primates) build freestanding shelters at all. Language is not basic; it is derived. It rests on the same underlying cognitive and social skills that lead infants to point to things and show things to other people declaratively and informatively, in a way that other primates do not do, and that lead them to engage in collaborative and joint attentional activities with others of a kind that are also unique among primates.

Tomasello and colleagues describe this infrastructure as 'shared intentionality': motivations and abilities to engage with others in cooperative, collaborative activities with shared goals, plans, and intentions, and to share attention, experiences, and other psychological states with others (Tomasello et al. 2005). It is this shared intentionality infrastructure that non-human primates lack, and which explains the difference between human language acquisition and the performance of language-trained apes and animal communication systems in the wild: 'What they lack are the skills and motivations of shared intentionality – such things as joint attention, perspective-taking and cooperative motives – for adjusting their communicative acts for others pragmatically, or for learning symbols whose main function is pragmatic' (Tomasello 2017: 95).

In more recent work, Tomasello and colleagues further elaborate their system for capturing the sociocognitive differences between humans and other apes and the development of shared intentionality in human children. Specifically, they distinguish between joint intentionality on the one hand and collective intentionality on the other. Joint intentionality is a second-personal, interactive mode in which infants and young children base their communication especially on their interlocutor's attentional, intentional, and knowledge states. This is children's mode of engagement before age three. Starting around age three, children develop an understanding of 'collective intentionality'. They begin to understand that conventions are based on collective agreements that guide and normatively coordinate social behaviour. This understanding of collective conventions is evident in children's complex sociocognitive behaviours, such as emerging concerns for social evaluation, impression management, and the enforcement of social norms (Engelmann et al. 2012; Tomasello 2014). It also scaffolds children's understanding of other linguistic behaviours based on the creation of interactional conventions, such as conceptual pacts (Matthews et al. 2010), pretend play (Pleyer 2020), and politeness and impoliteness norms (Pleyer & Pleyer 2016, 2022).

Animals, especially non-human primates, also exhibit complex social cognition (Seyfarth & Cheney 2015). For example, chimpanzees understand seeing, knowledge, and ignorance. They also know that others make inferences and understand others' goals, perceptions, and intentions (see, e.g., Call & Tomasello 2008; Bettle & Rosati 2021 for reviews). Current research even indicates that the controversial question 'Does the chimpanzee have a theory of mind?' (Premack & Woodruff 1978), that is, whether they can attribute mental states to others, can be answered with a yes.

Research with eighteen-month-old human infants has shown that they can generalise their own perceptual experience to the experience of others. In a study by Meltzoff and Brooks (2008), two groups of infants had experience with two different kinds of blindfolds. In one group, it was an opaque blindfold. But in the other group, it was a trick blindfold that looked opaque from the outside but was actually see-through. Infants in the opaque blindfold condition expected a person not to see an object when wearing it, whereas children in the see-through condition expected a person to be able to see the object. Follow-up research showed that children also used this experience to calculate what a person knew. In an experiment by Senju et al. (2011), eighteen-month-olds saw a typical 'false belief' test in which an object was first placed into a box by a teddy bear but then was taken out of the box again. Crucially, an adult shown watching the scene put on a blindfold after the object was put into the box. Eye-tracking showed that infants having experience with the opaque blindfold expected the adult to reach for the toy where they had seen the teddy bear put it. But infants having experience with the trick blindfold had no such expectation, as generalising from their own experience indicated that the adult had seen the toy being removed. Interestingly, Kano et al. (2019) replicated this study with chimpanzees, bonobos, and orangutans, who had experienced either an opaque barrier or a trick, see-through barrier. Eye-tracking data showed that most of the apes expected the adult to reach for the item in the box only in the opaque barrier condition but not in the trick barrier condition.

This question of theory of mind is of particular relevance because theory of mind and other related aspects of social cognition are intricately connected to specifically human communication making use of ostension, inference, and the recognition and expression of intentions. These capacities, then, are also argued to be crucial for the evolution of language (e.g., Tomasello 2008; Heintz & Scott-Phillips 2023). However, mastery of a more complex theory of mind seems to rely to some degree on children acquiring language and their enculturation in linguistic interactions (e.g., Astington & Baird 2005), suggesting a more complex co-evolutionary picture (Rubio-Fernandez 2023).

Overall, great apes show sophisticated sociocognitive skills, and the recognition and expression of intentions seem to be part of the evolutionary platform for the evolution of human language (Moore 2017). However, there still seem to be crucial differences between great ape social cognition and motivations and those of humans. Specifically, non-human primates show evidence of complex social cognition mostly in competitive contexts. For example, their understanding (and production) of declarative pointing seems to be extremely limited (though see Leavens et al. 2009). As mentioned, fourteen-month-olds understand a pointing gesture as informative for the question of which of two locations hides a toy. Chimpanzees, on the other hand, 'follow the point to the bucket and say, in effect, "A bucket. So what? Now where's the food?" They do not understand that the pointing is intended to be 'relevant' to the searching as a shared activity' (Tomasello & Carpenter 2007: 122).

Interestingly, in a similar context, when an experimenter makes a prohibitive gesture towards a bucket and then leaves the room, chimpanzees are able to infer a competitive motive and become interested in this bucket, and not the other (Herrmann & Tomasello 2006). They also become interested in a location if they see a chimpanzee try to reach towards it, as opposed to when a human experimenter points at it (Hare & Tomasello 2004). Bettle and Rosati (2021), along similar lines as Tomasello and colleagues, propose that other primates possess complex social cognition for competition. They argue that humans share this sociocognitive platform with other primates, but that humans have evolved additional social cognition for cooperation, which includes joint attention, sustained attention to others, attributing cooperative and shared intentions, and complex cooperative perspective-taking. This sociocognitive infrastructure for cooperation has been argued to represent a foundational, 'species-unique contribution to the language acquisition process' (Ibbotson 2020: 116). Another important aspect of this sociocognitive infrastructure for cooperation is that it includes a propensity for cultural learning and cumulative cultural evolution (Tomasello 1999), of which language evolution and change are prime examples (Pleyer 2023). Cumulative cultural evolution, based on the cooperative infrastructure for cooperation, therefore seems to be a foundational process in how language evolved.

However, it has to be noted here that a focus on shared intentionality and its relation to cultural evolution is 'not the only game in town'. The question of which (socio)cognitive abilities are the foundation of cultural evolution is very much an active field of research (see, e.g., Heyes & Moore 2023). The same holds for the question of how cultural evolution in turn transforms our cognitive processes, and leads to the emergence of new cognitive mechanisms which in turn influence cultural evolution in a dynamic feedback loop. For example, one such feedback loop that has been investigated concerns the way that language and social cognition co-develop and co-evolve (Rubio-Fernandez 2023).

One way to investigate how cultural evolution can lead to the emergence of structure, and the factors influencing this process, is experimentally. Indeed, the cultural evolution of language has increasingly been tested in laboratory settings. We will discuss this research in the next section.

5 Language Evolution in the Lab

While studies comparing humans and non-human animals as reviewed in Sections 2–4 can give valuable clues to the evolutionary scaffolding of language, it does not answer the question of how linguistic structure comes about over the course of cultural evolution. Although the diachronic development of existing languages (see Section 6) can prove informative here, it is hardly sufficient as we are dealing with fully fledged human languages that have developed over generations. In the absence of any records of the earliest stages of language, laboratory experiments are used to approximate situations in which, in one way or another, communicative systems are created from scratch. In this section, we give an overview over two of the most influential paradigms that investigate the evolution of human symbolic communication systems in laboratory settings: experimental semiotics on the one hand, and artificial language learning studies on the other. These two approaches overlap to some extent and have been combined in many ways, especially in recent research. Section 5.1 introduces experimental semiotics; Section 5.2 discusses Iterated Learning (IL) as arguably the most influential artificial language learning paradigm; Section 5.3 reviews more recent developments in experimental approaches investigating the different factors that shape the evolution of communication systems.

5.1 Experimental Semiotics and the Evolution of Language

One of the central questions in the evolution of language is the 'symbol grounding' problem (Harnad 1990; cf. Nölle & Galantucci 2022). That is, how did the first symbols emerge, and how were they connected to their referents? One experimental design that has been used to shed light on this question is experimental semiotics. Experimental semiotics is an influential paradigm to investigate how interactants can bootstrap a communication system and interactively co-create novel, structured symbol systems (see, e.g., Galantucci et al. 2012; Galantucci 2017; Nölle & Galantucci 2022). In this design, participants are not allowed to use language but instead have to solve a communicative problem without a pre-established communication system. Tasks usually fall into two domains: *referential communication games* and *coordination games*. In referential communication games, participants have to communicate about a set of referents. In coordination games, participants have to coordinate movements in an artificial environment. Overall, in both tasks, over repeated interactions, participants successfully negotiate meaningful symbols to communicate about referents, coordinate their actions, and converge on a shared communication system. Researchers then systematically change the design properties of these tasks along various dimensions in order to tease apart the different variables influencing the emergence of communication systems (see Delliponti et al. 2023 for a review). For example, they had participants use different channels and modalities of communication, for example, by using graphical symbols, drawing, gesture, or pantomime.

For instance, in a Pictionary-like task, participants had to draw referents, which then needed to be guessed by the other participant (Garrod et al. 2007). Here, drawings of referents such as 'Clint Eastwood' were first drawn in much detail based on iconic characteristics (e.g., by drawing a cowboy). But over repeated iterations of these games, once the referent had been successfully identified, the drawing would become more structured, as well as more abstract, and easier to guess (e.g., by just drawing a hat shape and a cigarette shape). These studies have shown that humans develop systematic communication systems in which they first create signs (form/meaning mappings), which become more systematic and con-ventionalised over time. However, 'it is unclear where this human propensity for systematicity comes from and how specific features are selected and become expressed in systematic categories' (Nölle et al. 2018). The emergence of novel communication systems in experimental semiotics is thought to be influenced by: (a) contextual factors (i.e., the potential associative connections between different sets of referents that are inherent in the environment), (b) cognitive factors (i.e., the ability to form associative links between sets of referents based on factors such as metaphoric mapping, analogy, indexicality, metonymic links, and so forth), and (c) semiotic resources assumed to be shared between interlocutors. For example, in Garrod et al. (2007), one final graphical symbol for Clint Eastwood was an arrow pointing right in a circle, which had emerged from an earlier strategy mixing iconic properties with a rebus-like method. Specifically, a participant drew not only the face of a cowboy but also four arrows arranged in the cardinal directions, with the eastern direction being circled. This property then became systematised and conventionalised as the novel graphical symbol for Clint Eastwood.

Interestingly, this reliance on shared semiotic and cultural resources indicates that enculturation and shared knowledge are important in these kinds of ground-ing processes. Indeed, Lister et al. (2020, 2021) showed that younger children (six years), who are less enculturated and had a smaller shared pool of concep-tual and cultural knowledge, were less successful in comprehending and creat-ing novel signs in the gestural and vocal modality than older children (twelve years) and adults. From the perspective of the evolution of language, this means that we have to be careful in interpreting results from experimental semiotics as they are done with human participants who know language, and share a rich pool of cultural knowledge. The same would not be the case for the initial emergence of symbolic communication in the hominin lineage.[6]

---

[6] The term *hominin* is used to refer to members 'of the group that includes humans and our extinct relatives' in the human lineage (Langdon 2022: 6).

Lister et al. (2020, 2021) – as well as other studies (e.g., Fay et al. 2014) – also found that participants generally are more successful in creating a communication system from scratch using gestures when compared to using vocalisations. These results are of particular interest regarding the question of whether the origins of language lie primarily in the gestural or vocal modality (e.g., Wacewicz & Żywiczyński 2017). However, we should see this in the context that both animal and human communication are fundamentally multimodal in character, which means that the origins of language very likely were also multimodal (e.g., Levinson & Holler 2014). The question then becomes what the specific contributions are of the gestural and vocal modalities, as well as their interactions. Indeed, Macuch Silva et al. (2020) found that participants only using the gestural modality in a referential communication task were as accurate as those who could use multimodal signals. However, they found that multimodality conferred an efficiency advantage, meaning that they were faster at conveying a stimulus to a partner.

Overall, experimental semiotics shows that humans can create systematic and structured novel symbol systems without language. However, the cognitive mechanisms involved in this still need to be better understood. In addition, they mainly concern a relatively small shared symbolic storage of associations. Interactions also happen over a comparatively short time frame, which therefore does not adequately capture the multigenerational dynamics of the emergence of structure in historical language change (Nölle & Galantucci 2022). This is what we are going to turn to next.

5.2 Iterated Learning: Computational Approaches and Behavioural Experiments

As a cultural artefact, language is transmitted from generation to generation. This is what the term *iterated learning* refers to: each generation of learners acquires language by experiencing linguistic input from other people who have learned the language before. But the term *iterated learning* has also come to refer to an approach that operationalizes this fundamental process of generational transmission via computer simulations or in the laboratory. Iterated learning is an approach that has proven particularly successful in language evolution research – in fact, scientometric analyses of abstracts from the pertinent conferences in the field have shown that it is among the most central topics in the field (e.g., Bergmann & Dale 2016; Wacewicz et al. 2023b). The IL model was pioneered in Kirby's (2001) seminal computational simulation. But the most well-known and most widely cited IL study is probably that of Kirby et al. (2008), which pioneered the use of the IL framework in laboratory studies with human participants. As the authors themselves acknowledge, their study was not without precedent, though: Bartlett (1932) and Bavelas (1952) had already used laboratory communication experiments for their studies of human memory, and as Nölle and Galantucci (2022: 66) point out, early attempts to study language change using miniature artificial languages can already be found in the 1920s and 1930s (Esper 1925; Wolfle 1933; see also Christiansen & Chater 2022 for discussion). Also, a number of communication game studies had already used repeated interactions between pairs of participants (Garrod & Doherty 1994; Galantucci 2005; Garrod et al. 2007; Selten & Warglien 2007; see Section 5.1). The main innovation of Kirby et al.'s approach was that they explicitly addressed the question of whether a structured language can emerge from unstructured stimuli without intentional design in an experimental setting.

Kirby et al.'s study consisted of two experiments using largely the same design, with the second one introducing a minor modification. In the first experiment, participants learned an 'alien' language that consisted of written labels (the signal space) and pictures of coloured objects in motion (the meaning space[7]). Importantly, they were only trained on a subset of the stimuli set that constituted the miniature language (the SEEN set). In the subsequent testing phase, in which participants were presented with pictures and asked to produce the correct label in the 'alien' language, they were tested on the SEEN and UNSEEN sets in their entirety. The results of this experiment showed a decrease in transmission error over the different generations, as well as an increase in compositionality. Transmission error was assessed using a measure of string similarity (edit distances), while compositionality was assessed by measuring the correlation between pairs of edit distances on the one hand and the Hamming distance between pairs of meanings on the other, the latter quantifying the number of features in which the meanings differed (i.e., meanings differing in one feature had a distance of 1, meanings differing in two features a distance of 2, etc.). Taken together, these results suggest that the miniature languages evolved to become more structured. More specifically, the languages develop systematic underspecification: as there is a 'bottleneck on transmission' (Kirby et al. 2008: 10685) because some of the items were held back from the participants during the training phase, there is no way for them to rote-learn all meanings. Instead, they have to make systematic generalisations. For example, in one of the miniature languages in their data, the string *tuge* comes to refer to all objects that move horizontally, regardless of whether they are circles, squares, or triangles.

---

[7] The terms *signal space* and *meaning space* are not used in Kirby et al. (2008) but are common in other IL studies (e.g., Verhoef et al. 2016; Little et al. 2017).

The second experiment made a minor modification in order to test the role of the pressure for expressivity: before each participant's training, the SEEN set was filtered in such a way that if any strings were assigned to more than one meaning, all but one of those meanings were removed from the training data. This 'effectively removes the possibility of the language adapting to be learnable by introducing underspecification: filtering ensures that underspecification is an evolutionary dead-end' (Kirby et al. 2008: 10684). The results again showed a clear and significant decrease in transmission error. And even though the evolution of underspecification was blocked by the experimental set-up, the measure of compositionality indicated that the languages became increasingly structured over time. A more qualitative analysis of the data leads the authors to the conclusion that what we see here is the evolution of structure *within* the signals. For instance, one of the miniature languages evolves three distinct morphemes expressing colour, shape, and movement, respectively.

In their discussion of the results, Kirby et al. (2008) particularly focus on the role of compositionality, which, they argue, optimises the competing constraints for learnability/efficiency and expressivity. The evolution of compositionality over the course of IL can be seen as an adaptive response to the pressures imposed by the 'transmission bottleneck' that exists between the producer and the learner (Kirby et al. 2008: 10685).

Kirby et al.'s (2008) seminal study has inspired a large number of follow-up experiments.

5.3 Recent Developments in Artificial Language Learning Experiments

The IL paradigm has been used extensively in studies on the cultural evolution of language (for reviews, see, e.g., Tamariz 2014, 2017). Instead of giving a full overview, we focus on a few selected studies that arguably illustrate key developments in the application of the paradigm. For one thing, the IL paradigm has been extended to more modalities. For example, Verhoef (2012) trained participants on artificial languages that were produced with slide whistles, thus introducing a 'speech' apparatus that involves less interference from previous experience with spoken language. Just like the written-language stimuli in Kirby et al.'s (2008) experiment, the whistle systems became more learnable and more structured over the generations. Motamedi et al. (2021) combine a silent gesture paradigm with IL to examine the emergence of systematic argument marking beyond word order, showing that participants converge on different strategies to disambiguate clause arguments, which become more consistent over the course of transmission.

Kempe et al. (2015, 2019) as well as Raviv and Arnon (2018) compared the performance of adults and children in IL studies. Kempe et al. (2015) show that in the iterated transmission of random dot patterns, transmission accuracy increased to a similar extent in five- to eight-year-old children and in adults; also, structure emerged more readily in the children, which may have to do with the fact that the children tended to introduce more radical innovations that reduced complexity in earlier generations, which led to structures that were more easily transmissible (Kempe et al. 2015: 251). Kempe et al. (2019), using auditory stimuli, showed that in a dyadic referential communication game, only adults but not children were able to converge on an iconic and structured system, which leads them to the conclusion that the emergence and transmission of linguistic systems are unlikely to be driven by child learners. This also has implications for theories of language change (see Section 6.1), as some accounts of linguistic change assign a key role to children. Raviv and Arnon (2018), working with written stimuli like the ones used by Kirby et al. (2008), showed that both adults and seven- to twelve-year-old children introduced structured ambiguities, but only adults showed evidence of introducing compositional structure. Also, they showed that the adults significantly outperformed the children in learning the artificial languages despite having the same or less exposure. They hypothesise that children may have weaker biases for structure, and/or 'children's difficulty in learning the artificial language may have affected their ability to regularize and introduce structure' (Raviv & Arnon 2018: 171).

But apart from extending the paradigm to new modalities or groups of participants, follow-up studies have tested more complex hypotheses, often combining IL and experimental semiotics (Tamariz 2017: 392).

Kirby et al. (2015: 85), reviewing a number of previous IL studies, summarise their results as follows: a pressure for compressibility arising from transmission to new learners results in degenerate languages (if it is not counterbalanced by a pressure for expressivity); a pressure for expressivity arising from communication leads to holistic systems; a pressure from both communication and transmission leads to structure – but the same effect can be achieved via generational transmission and an artificial pressure against degeneracy. The term 'degeneracy' in this context means that different meanings are associated with the same signal that is therefore maximally ambiguous (note that the term is used differently in other contexts; according to Van de Velde 2014, degeneracy refers to the phenomenon that different elements can fulfil the same function). But especially in the last ten years or so, many more factors that go beyond such more or less system-internal pressures have been taken into account.

In particular, several studies have focused on the role of *context* in the evolution of artificial miniature languages. Silvey et al. (2015) used a modified version of Kirby et al.'s (2008) original paradigm, systematically backgrounding one meaning dimension (e.g., colour, shape, or movement pattern). They trained participants on an artificial language, but with each label, they showed the participants *two* images instead of one, with one image being a distractor. Importantly, the two pictures shared one consistent dimension, that is, attending to this dimension would never help participants to discriminate between the two meanings. Their main result is that the patterns of underspecification that emerged in the transmission process reflected the salience of the different dimensions in learning and production contexts. The languages lost distinctions earlier and faster in the dimension that was consistently backgrounded (Silvey et al. 2015: 222).

Tinits et al. (2017) used a similar experimental set-up but focused on the emergence of overspecification instead of underspecification. The meaning space in this experiment consisted of four different objects (pen, book, ball, and cup) in two different colours (yellow and blue). Participants were trained on a minimally specified language, which means that, for example, the colour dimension was only specified when it was necessary to disambiguate the target object from the distractor object. In the test phase, participants were assigned to one of two conditions: in the simple-context condition, only one single object was displayed in each test trial. In the complex-context condition, two different objects were shown in each test trial. The results show that the two contexts lead to considerably different developments: in the complex-context condition, in which the relevant meaning dimensions are harder to discern, the trend towards overspecification (i.e., specifying a meaning dimension that is not relevant in the current context) is stronger.

The studies by Silvey et al. (2015) and Tinits et al. (2017) illustrate a broader trend in the development of artificial language learning studies. While earlier studies had mainly focused on transmission – sometimes taking communication into account by integrating elements of communication games as pioneered in experimental semiotics – several studies have focused on the role of the communicative contexts. Following up on Silvey et al. (2015), Winters et al. (2015) contrasted various configurations of referential contexts. They found the resulting language to mark idiosyncratic elements of the figures, just one systematic dimension, or both the idiosyncratic and the systematic dimensions based on the configuration used in IL. Another follow-up study manipulated the predictability of the referential context and found that systematic and compositional marking was most likely to emerge when the content of the referential context was most unpredictable (Winters et al. 2018). The authors interpret this in terms of signal autonomy: as a result of the lack of information in context, linguistic signals adapt to become usable in any context.

Raviv et al. (2019) argue that pressures for expressivity and compressibility are already present during real-world communication, and that compositionality can emerge without the need for generational transmission. To test this hypothesis, they tested six 'micro-societies', each consisting of four participants, who communicated in alternating pairs using an artificial language to refer to an expanding meaning space. The results showed that the languages became significantly more structured over several rounds of interaction, and that they developed compositionality even in the absence of generational transmission. Also, the languages became more consistent and more communicatively successful over the different rounds of interaction. In discussing their results, Raviv et al. (2019: 162) point out that the finding that compositionality can emerge within the first generation is in line with observations made in the development of real-world languages, such as emerging sign languages (see Section 6.2).

In general, it seems fair to say that the focus has slightly shifted from IL experiments that mainly focus on transmission to communication-game designs that take other, for example, environmental, factors into account. Nölle et al. (2018), for example, use a silent-gesture paradigm to investigate how environmental factors influence the development of structure in emerging communication systems, showing that 'systematic structure emerges in response to broader environmental and contextual affordances' (Nölle et al. 2018: 103). One domain in which environmental affordances play a crucial role is spatial language, as has been shown in research on real-world languages (Levinson 2003). In a series of experiments in which natural language data were elicited, Nölle et al. (2020a, 2020b) have investigated the role of environmental affordances in the development of spatial language using different strategies: on the one hand, Nölle et al. (2020a) use a variant of the maze game pioneered by Garrod and Anderson (1987), in which participants have to collaboratively coordinate in a maze. In Nölle et al.'s adaptation of the experiment, the mazes differed in their shape. Analysing the written chat that the participants used to coordinate, Nölle et al. (2020a) show that the participants were highly sensitive to the affordances of the particular environment. More specifically, they used different communicative strategies, for example, a 'figural' one when confronted with a maze that had a highly irregular shape, drawing on expressions like *an indent* or *the branch*, while they conceptualised the maze as consisting of rows and columns when it was presented in a 'stratified' way, using expressions like *the third row from the bottom*. Nölle et al. (2020b) used a virtual reality (VR) set-up to compare the communicative strategies that players of a VR game would use when coordinating their positions in different kinds of environments, showing that depending on the structure of the VR landscape, participants preferred egocentric (*left*; *right*) or allocentric (*across the river*; *behind the mountain*) frames of reference. While these experiments work with natural language, they show that the contexts in which we use language strongly influence how exactly we use it, which can potentially entail differences in linguistic structure.

These experimental approaches can also shed light on the phenomena that have been discussed in cognitive linguistics and beyond under the label of 'linguistic relativity'. In the broadest terms, linguistic relativity refers to the idea that the language(s) we use have an impact on the way we think (see, e.g., Gumperz & Levinson 1996; Everett 2013). For example, different languages have different ways of conceptualising the spatial relation between objects (e.g., egocentric vs. allocentric: *the tree is in front of the house* vs. *the tree is to the south of the house*; see Levinson 2003: 28). This kind of variability in how different languages construe the world has also been shown to lead to behavioural differences in experimental set-ups, which indicates that different linguistic construals may shape our conceptualisation of the world (see Everett 2013 and Lucy 2016 for reviews). That is, by learning a particular language, the cognitive system becomes trained to pay attention to conceptual categories 'that have evolved over historical time in the community' (Verhagen 2021: 55). From the perspective of evolutionary cognitive linguistics, the adaptation of linguistic conventions to their environment and linguistic relativity can be seen as two sides of the same coin. The perspectival construal patterns that constitute the linguistic repertoire of language users emerge as 'socio-cultural conventions stabilised through processes of cultural evolution' (Nölle et al. 2020) and are the result of recurring coordination and perspectivation efforts of previous generations of interactants within particular communities (Tomasello 1999; see also Steels & Belpaeme 2005). Once they have been established, they necessarily influence individual cognition and behaviour. This holds especially when construing conceptual content for purposes of expression in a way that is congruent with what previous generations of language users have found relevant (cf. Slobin's 1996 idea of 'Thinking for Speaking'). This is the case because memorising situations and events with respect to the conceptual categories encoded within a particular language facilitates talking about these situations and events in ways that are relevant to a particular linguistic community (Verhagen 2021: 55).

In recent work, the IL paradigm, as well as artificial language learning paradigms more generally, have also been used to address typological questions (Levshina 2018) or, using computational modelling (Ito & Feldman 2022) or communication game experiments (Ventura et al. 2022), for investigating historical language change. In addition, some communication game studies have significantly increased the pool of participants by drawing on online interfaces or even on smartphone apps (Morin et al. 2018, 2022).

Recent work has also adopted a sociolinguistic perspective. For instance, Fedzechkina et al. (2023) combine artificial language learning by addressing how social biases can influence language structure. They trained participants on a miniature language with two 'dialects', one employing case, the other not. In one condition, the participants were socially biased towards users of one of the two dialects: they were told that 'We are especially keen to trade with the blue aliens. They seem to be on our side, and they have important resources. We should try to impress these blue aliens in particular' (Fedzechkina et al. 2023: 6). Interestingly, learners biased towards users of the no-case dialect tended to drop case even if case was informative, thus creating a linguistic system with high message uncertainty. This suggests that biases such as the pressures for expressivity and efficiency interact with social biases, and that in some cases the latter can even override the former. While this overview is by no means exhaustive, the examples discussed in this section show that experimental approaches using artificial miniature languages have managed to capture a large set of factors that influence linguistic structure. This has led Roberts (2017) to call experiments in language change 'the linguist's drosophila', referring to the fly species that has been used widely in genetic research, that is, a way to observe change in the laboratory that can then be used to make generalisations about dynamics of change in modern languages.

While some questions regarding the ecological validity of laboratory experiments (as well as computational modelling approaches, which we have largely neglected here) remain open, many of the results obtained in such controlled settings are highly compatible with the dynamics that can be observed in natural languages.

6 Real-World Language Dynamics: What Language Emergence and Change Reveal about Evolution

As mentioned in Section 1, to what extent the dynamics observed in present-day languages can be subsumed under the umbrella term 'language evolution' is an open question. But especially if we take a usage-based perspective on language evolution (see Section 7), the cultural evolution of language is at least as important as the evolutionary developments that led to the emergence of the cognitive mechanisms underlying the human capacity for language, especially given the assumption that both are closely intertwined, and that at least some of the cognitive principles that underlie language use and language dynamics in the present must have played a role in the biological evolution of the human capacity for language. As such, analysing variation and change in present-day languages can prove insightful for understanding processes of cultural evolution. In the subsequent sections, we will mostly focus on research that has been conducted in the framework of Construction Grammar, which in turn has been singled out as a highly promising approach for studying language evolution by multiple authors (e.g., Arbib 2012; Hurford 2012; Johansson 2016; Hartmann & Pleyer 2021). But this focus on Construction Grammar does not mean that other cognitive-linguistic approaches could not offer equally relevant insights. To mention just one recent example, Schmid's (2020) entrenchment-and-conventionalisation model, which synthesises elements from multiple influential cognitive-linguistic approaches, can be considered a promising overarching framework for studies on language evolution as well.

6.1 Evolutionary Perspectives on Language Variation and Change

While questions from the domain of historical linguistics have long been seen as outside the scope of language evolution research, recent developments in the field suggest that their importance for understanding cultural evolution is acknowledged to an increasing extent. This is shown, for example, by the growing number of presentations for this domain at the most important conferences in the field (see, e.g., Gong et al. 2014: 508; Wacewicz et al. 2023b). Importantly, the relationship between language evolution research and historical linguistics can be seen as a bilateral one: on the one hand, insights from historical linguistics can prove relevant for language evolution research in that they reveal general processes of cultural evolution; on the other hand, accounts of language change make use of evolutionary concepts to account for historical processes (e.g., Croft 2000; see also Harder 2010). In this section, we discuss selected examples of approaches to language variation and change that apply evolutionary ideas – in particular, the generalised theory of evolution as developed by Hull (1988) – to the study of language change. Firstly, we take a closer look at Croft's (2000) framework, which borrows many ideas from evolutionary biology. Secondly, we briefly introduce Ritt's (2004) framework, which is rooted in a generalised theory of evolution. Thirdly, we take a closer look at one specific phenomenon of crucial importance for understanding language change from an evolutionary point of view, namely competition.

While Croft (2000) is perhaps the monograph that makes the connection between language change and evolutionary theory most explicit, it is not without its precursors. Evolutionary theories of language change have a long history that can be traced back at least to Schleicher (1863), who argued that his own theory of language change, which views languages as 'natural organisms', is an instance of Darwinian evolution. Also, various linguists working on language change in the second half of the twentieth century have explicitly drawn on evolutionary concepts, after evolutionary metaphors or analogy had fallen out of fashion for a fairly long time (McMahon 1994: 314). Keller (1994: 191–215), for instance, explicitly frames language change as an evolutionary process, drawing on Dawkins' (2006) notion of cultural replicators (memes). Lass (1990) famously adapted the evolutionary concept of exaptation to linguistics, which has become an important explanatory device in explaining how existing linguistic units can take on new functions.

What distinguishes Croft's approach from previous ones is that he develops a fairly comprehensive evolutionary account of language change. Adopting Hull's (1988) generalised theory of evolution, he develops a 'Theory of Utterance Selection' in which selection processes in biology and language are conceived of as different instantiations of more general selection processes. 'Linguemes' are conceived of as replicators, in analogy to genes in biology, while utterances are seen as structured sets of replicators, analogous to strings of DNA in biology. In this view, language evolution is seen as a process of variation and selection, in which innovations are introduced through a variety of mechanisms (as it is introduced by recombination or mutation of genes in biological evolution), which leads to the emergence of variants (analogous to alleles in biology), and ultimately to the selection of variants via entrenchment of conventions by speakers and its propagation in communication (Croft 2000: 38). However, Croft (2000: 39–40) also points out important disanalogies between linguistic and biological evolution. For one thing, while altered replication of genes through recombination of DNA or, more rarely, mutation is a more or less random process, external functional motivation seems to be the much more common causal factor for altered replication. Secondly, the relationship between replicator and interactor is different: in biology, the replicator, as the genotype, 'produces' the interactor, that is, the phenotype (the organism); in language, it is the interactor who 'produces' the utterance, that is, the replicator. He argues, however, that this has no bearing on the mechanisms involved in replication, interaction, and evolution (Croft 2000: 40).

Ritt (2004) takes a similar approach in that he also draws on a generalised theory of evolution, or 'universal Darwinism' (Ritt 2004: 116). While Croft's approach is strongly based on Hull (1988), Ritt's concept relies more on Dawkins (2006), as the title of his monograph ('Selfish Sounds and Linguistic Evolution') already reveals. He explicitly embraces the idea of conceptualising languages as a complex adaptive system, rather than conceiving of a language as an essentially static and passive system of knowledge (Ritt 2004: 17). Similar to Croft, he points out a number of analogies and disanalogies between biological and linguistic evolution (Ritt 2004: 89–91). As for the former, he argues, for example, that languages, like organisms, are complex and functional; as for disanalogies, one of the main points he mentions is that language users are conscious, while biological evolution is 'blind'. Focusing on sound change, Ritt (2004: 120) argues that evolutionary changes in language can be predicted in replicator systems, which entails that the most adequate way of approaching language change involves three questions: '(a) what the replicating units that constitute competences actually are, (b) by what mechanics they replicate, and (c) what (environmental) factors influence their success at replicating' (Ritt 2004: 121). In one case study, he applies this theoretical approach to Middle English vowel quantity. According to this approach, for example, short /a/ and long /a:/ can be thought of as replicators that compete for association to morphs, with /a/ initially being associated with morphological forms like *have*, *make*, and *grase*, which gradually became more strongly associated with /a:/ instead (Ritt 2004: 257–259). Eventually, /a:/ ousted /a/ in open syllables (open syllable lengthening), while /a/ ended up prevailing in the case of *have* (Ritt 2004: 258).

Zehentner (2019) extends this approach to other phenomena of language change and combines it with a Construction Grammar perspective. In particular, she develops an evolutionary account of competition in language, partly drawing on Steels' (2011) evolutionary Construction Grammar approach. As the concepts of variation and selection are key to evolutionary approaches to language change, competition plays a crucial role in any such account, as the emergence of new variants necessarily leads to competition between different alternatives. Note that this is also one domain in which cognitive linguistics and particularly Construction Grammar can prove insightful for an understanding of linguistic evolution, as especially the latter has always been concerned with the study of 'alternations' (see Pijpops 2020 for some critical reflections on this term), for example, the so-called dative alternation (*I gave her the book – I gave the book to her*, see, e.g., Goldberg 1995). But while many individual alternations have been studied in much detail, an evolutionary perspective – as pointed out in Ritt's (2004) quote cited earlier in this section – entails the crucial question of what the general mechanisms behind such competition phenomena are, and what actually counts as competition.

Like Croft and Ritt, Zehentner (2019) uses the concept of replicators. But while Croft views *utterances* as the main unit of replication in language, Zehentner sees constructions, that is, form–meaning pairings at various levels of abstraction, as units of replication (replicators). Constructions change on a micro-level as language users introduce variation, which can lead to competition. Bauer et al. (2013: 33), focusing on processes of morphological rivalry, define competition as follows: 'Two processes compete when they both have the potential to be used in the coining of new synonymous forms from the same base'. Generalising this definition to other domains of grammar, we can speak of competition when different patterns that fulfil the same functions can be used (partly) interchangeably. Importantly, whether any two processes compete or not cannot always be answered categorically. In many cases, there may be partial rivalry between different constructions showing functional overlap in some domains but not others (Guzmán Naranjo & Bonami 2023). Also, newly emerged constructions can compete with previously unrelated patterns, especially if two constructions overlap in meaning (Zehentner 2019: 301).

In a Construction Grammar framework, functionally similar patterns can be conceived of as being connected via 'synonymy links' (Goldberg 1995: 91), and they can be seen as 'allostructions' (Cappelle 2006). Once a new competitor enters the network, the links to other constructions can gradually become stronger or weaker, depending on various factors like the contexts in which they occur, their usage frequency, and potentially also the degree to which they 'stand out' in comparison to other constructions, for example, via the use of 'extravagant' formal means such as repetition, unusual phoneme combinations, or (apparent) violation of grammatical rules (see, e.g., Haspelmath 1999; Ungerer & Hartmann 2020).

Recent work in diachronic Construction Grammar has focused on the question of how overarching patterns of competition between constructions can be modelled. De Smet et al. (2018) distinguish a number of ways in which competing forms change their functions: in the case of substitution, only one form survives – for instance, they argue that *-ing* clauses may currently be in the process of substituting *to*-infinitives after *begin* in American English (*begin to work > begin working*; De Smet et al. 2018: 207). Differentiation, by contrast, refers to the phenomenon of competing constructions coming to occupy different functional niches. For instance, they show that [*start* + *-ing*-clause] and [*start* + *to*-infinitive] rarely combined with non-agentive subjects until the 1990s in American English. Recent data show, however, that both constructions opened up for non-agentive subjects, but this trend is much more pronounced for [*start* + *to*-infinitive]. Finally, attraction refers to the phenomenon of two constructions becoming functionally more, rather than less, alike. Again, [*begin* + *-ing*-clause] and [*begin* + *to*-infinitive] can be seen as an example of this, according to De Smet et al. (2018: 211): while a purely frequency-based comparison suggests a relation of substitution, a closer inspection of how each form is used also suggests that the two constructions grow more similar – while [*become* + *-ing*-clause] becomes more permissive of non-agentive subjects, [*begin* + *to*-infinitive] starts to combine with agentive subjects more frequently.

Using evolutionary linguistics as an explanatory framework, Zehentner (2019) emphasises that in her approach, evolutionary concepts are not just used metaphorically but instead 'competition between linguistic variants is thought to be fundamentally subject to the same general evolutionary mechanisms as biological ones' (Zehentner 2019: 277). This is very much in line with the generalised theory of evolution adopted, in slightly different ways, by Croft and Ritt, and that has become increasingly popular not only in linguistics but also in many other areas of scientific inquiry, culminating in the rise of cultural evolution as an academic field in its own right (Creanza et al. 2017; Lewens & Buskell 2023). The question to what degree evolutionary concepts are used in a metaphorical or analogical way, and to what degree biological and cultural evolution are actually seen as instances of the same processes is answered differently in different approaches. As mentioned earlier in this section, Croft (2000), for example, points out a number of disanalogies between linguistic and biological evolution but argues that such differences do not weaken the generalised theory of evolution – instead, he argues that a generalised theory of evolution only specifies certain causal relationships between replicator, interactor, and environment but otherwise affords many variations in the specific causal relationships that hold between these entities in different manifestations of evolution in different domains.

While most of the approaches summarised in the present section so far focus on the question of how evolutionary concepts can be applied to explaining changes in the traceable history of human languages, the assumption that language evolution is a special case of cultural evolution also allows for extending the findings that have been obtained in the traceable history to the more distant past. To some extent, this is, of course, a tool that has been used fruitfully in historical linguistics for a long time for mostly descriptive purposes: the so-called comparative method has been used to reconstruct earlier stages of existing languages and hypothesised protolanguages (used in the sense of 'precursor languages' here, e.g., Proto-Indo-European as a precursor to the, e.g., Romance or Germanic language families, not in the sense in which is it used in language evolution research; see, e.g., Campbell 2013). But the reconstruction of prehistoric languages has been taken beyond the merely descriptive level in more recent research, and more explanatory research questions have taken centre stage (see, e.g., Benítez-Burraco & Progovac 2021). One research field that seems particularly promising for informing language evolution research is the study of grammaticalisation, that is, the emergence of (more) grammatical forms from (more) lexical ones (Hopper & Traugott 2003; Heine & Kuteva 2007). In line with Bybee's (2010) assumption (already cited in Section 1) that the first grammatical constructions must have emerged in the same ways as those observed in more recent history, the general mechanisms observed in grammaticalisation processes may have played a role in the emergence of fully fledged languages as well. Indeed, some of the processes observed in artificial language learning experiments actually resemble grammaticalisation processes. Lehmann (2015) has famously proposed six parameters of grammaticalisation, three of them pertaining to the paradigmatic organisation of a language system, the others to syntagmatic aspects: (a) integrity – grammaticalised signs often show phonological attrition, cf. *going to* > *gonna*, (b) paradigmaticity – the existence of clear-cut paradigmatic relations; for instance, tense or aspect categories form relatively small, coherent classes, while less strongly grammaticalised classes, for example, so-called secondary prepositions tend to be larger and less coherent, (c) paradigmatic variability, that is, the freedom that language users have in choosing a sign. Strongly grammaticalised categories are highly obligatory, that is, language users have to choose between, for example, present or past tense; the future tense, by contrast, is less strongly grammaticalised in many languages (if they even have one), which is why language users can often choose between future tense and futurate present in many languages. As for the syntagmatic parameters, Lehmann proposes (d) structural scope – for example, auxiliary *have* has a broader syntactic scope than the full verb *have* (*I have stolen a bike* vs. *I have a bike*, the former having scope over an entire proposition); (e) bondedness, that is, the degree to which a sign is connected to another sign, to the extent that they coalesce (cf. again *gonna*); (f) syntagmatic variability, that is, the ease with which a sign can be shifted in its context – for instance, definite articles have a fixed position (in English, at the beginning of an NP), while the position of other words is more flexible (see, e.g., Szczepaniak 2011: 20).

While only few experimental studies have explicitly addressed questions of grammaticalisation, some of the developments along the parameters proposed by Lehmann can be observed in the miniature languages that develop in artificial language learning studies. For example, the phenomenon that the use of specific signals becomes more obligatory over time, and the freedom of language users to choose between variants becomes more limited, can be observed in some IL studies (see, e.g., Tinits et al. 2017).

Taken together, experimental studies and the study of historical language change can complement each other in developing and testing hypotheses about the mechanisms underlying the emergence of linguistic structure (also see Hartmann & Pleyer 2020). Another complementary line of research is the investigation of developing sign languages, where we can also observe many of the processes that are typical for grammaticalisation. The next section gives a brief overview of this line of research.

6.2 From Gestures to Signs? The Case of 'Emerging' Sign Languages

Language evolution research has been informed in various ways by signed languages (e.g., Armstrong & Wilcox 2007). In recent years, one area that has received particular attention is that of 'emerging sign languages' (Brentari & Coppola 2013).

These are sign languages with a relatively short time depth of only a few generations since their emergence. One of the most well-publicised cases is that of Nicaraguan Sign Language (NSL), which emerged in Nicaragua in the 1980s when many deaf children were brought together in a school where they were supposed to learn lip-reading (Senghas et al. 2004). Signers brought their individual structured communicative practices with them (often referred to as 'homesign', but see Hou 2022 and references therein for a critical discussion of the term and the ideologies tied to it). But in the context of children interacting with each other in this school, a shared, conventionalised, and structured sign language emerged. It was subsequently transmitted to later generations of children as they entered school, developing further conventionalised grammatical structures in the process transmission and continuing daily use in everyday life (Meir et al. 2010; cf. Tomasello 2008). NSL is classified as an emerging urban sign language, but most emerging sign languages are rural or village sign languages, which often emerge in the context of a high incidence of deafness in the community (De Vos & Pfau 2015).

Emerging sign languages have been met with strong interest in language evolution research as a potential 'window into language evolution' (Mineiro et al. 2021). However, it has to be made clear that 'the sign languages of the world are used by human individuals living in human societies' (Pleyer et al. 2022). This is of special importance when taking a species-comparative and evolutionary perspective because emerging sign languages are just as much 'true' human languages as any others (cf. Zeshan & de Vos 2012). They represent the dynamic human activity of 'languaging' (Henner & Robinson 2023) and interactive, collaborative co-creation of meaning. Work on emerging languages in the past has been in danger of exoticising signing communities (Braithwaite 2020; Pleyer et al. 2022). Especially from an evolutionary perspective, it is therefore paramount not to characterise emerging sign languages as 'immature languages' closer to the emergence of language than more 'mature' languages. This view rests on problematic assumptions similar to the ones reflected in the notion of 'creole exceptionalism' (DeGraff 2003), which are partly based on colonialist and dehumanising ideologies of 'primitive' languages being used by 'primitive' people, in contrast to 'evolved' languages being used by 'evolved' people (DeGraff 2005). We have to be aware of the ideological dimensions of categories, such as 'emerging sign language', as they might be tied to ideological assumptions about what is and isn't language (Hou & de Vos 2022).

With this in mind, the study of emerging sign languages can be useful for studying the evolutionary dynamics involved in conventionalisation and transmission, as they possess highly relevant sociolinguistic and historical profiles for this question. As for a number of these languages, we can identify their point of origin in time, they offer a specific window into the pressures and dynamics that shape all living languages over time (see also Hou 2020; Pleyer et al. 2022). They can also elucidate the role in which these dynamics, community structure, and communicative practices interact with the unique specific sociohistorical contexts of each language.

One case to illustrate this is São Tomé and Príncipe Sign Language (LGSTP, Mineiro et al. 2017, 2021). São Tomé and Príncipe is a group of West African islands with about 220,000 inhabitants. The country has a high incidence of deafness (about 3%), many due to the effects of prophylactic Malaria medication during pregnancy. In 2012–2013, the humanitarian project 'Without Barriers' brought 100 deaf participants from ages four to twenty-five together to help them create their own sign language. They did so by providing them with the opportunity to interact with each other on a daily basis over the period of two years. These daily interactions, as well as structured sessions in which picture cards were used to elicit signs, led to the emergence, stabilisation, and conventionalisation of linguistic forms. Initial signs were mostly pantomimic, iconic, and holistic in character. But over time, signs have become more time efficient, and exhibited greater articulatory economy, a more clearly defined signing space, word order preferences, emerging compounding patterns, as well as a pronominal system based on pointing (as also found in other sign languages) (Mineiro et al. 2017, 2021). As any other living language, LGSTP is still in continuous development. While iconic signs currently dominate the lexicon, there is a clear drive towards arbitrariness, reduction of articulatory elements, and developing internal structure of signs. From the perspective of language evolution, LGSTP provides evidence for the potential of pantomime (Żywiczyński et al. 2018; Zlatev et al. 2020) and iconicity (Pleyer et al. 2017) in grounding communication systems (see Sections 5.2 and 5.3). However, it also shows how based on these foundations, cognitive, interactional, and community dynamics lead to the emergence of a mutually shared, symbolic, and structured communication system.

From a sociolinguistic perspective, possibly the most important aspect of the emergence of LGSTP is that it helped create a sense of community and belonging:

> Deaf people now meet outside the classroom, and one can often observe children, adolescents, and adults on the street communicating with each other with their hands. The fluidity of the communicative exchanges using LGSTP between them is remarkable. Deaf people in Sao Tome and Principe have become a community with a common characteristic: a language that unites them and through which they can communicate. (Mineiro et al. 2017: 12)

In sum, then, the development of these sign languages shows not only that many of the mechanisms that can be observed in other contexts, for example, in grammaticalisation as well as in the grounding of new communication systems in laboratory situations, seem to apply here as well, but it also lends further support to the key role of interaction and joint intentionality in the development of language.

7 A Usage-Based Perspective on the Evolution of Language

In this Element, we have discussed a number of key topics central to integrating cognitive linguistics and language evolution research. Through this, we have illustrated how both fields can enter into a productive dialogue. On the one hand, this concerns how cognitive linguistics can be informed by – and correlates with – research on language evolution, especially when it comes to research on (a) the cognitive and social foundations of language and interaction (Sections 2, 3, and 4), and (b) the evolutionary dynamics of the emergence of structure in language (Sections 5 and 6). On the other hand, it concerns how cognitive linguistics can inform the study of language evolution with regard to the key topics discussed here. Minimally, we have shown that these topics, as well as others, need to be integrated if we want to arrive at a cognitive-linguistic account of language evolution. The massively interdisciplinary nature of language evolution research of course makes this a highly complex undertaking. So while we have given a comprehensive overview of central topics from a perspective integrating cognitive linguistics and language evolution research, we have in essence still only scratched the surface of relevant topics where both fields can cross-fertilise each other.

Here, in conclusion, we want to adopt a broader perspective and show two principal ways in which cognitive linguistics and language evolution research can be integrated: one concerns the utility of cognitive linguistics in spelling out the foundations of language evolution. The other concerns the broader contribution of cognitive linguistics, usage-based approaches, and evolutionary linguistics to understanding language as a complex adaptive system.

The first principal way of integrating cognitive linguistics and language evolution research entails a kind of 'shopping list' approach where cognitive linguistics helps in outlining the cognitive and interactional mechanisms and processes that have to be present in a 'language-, interaction-, and construction-ready brain' (Arbib 2012; Pleyer 2023) in order to make the evolution of language possible. This includes, for example, the human ability for symbolic cognition, a capacity for massive storage of a network of constructions in memory, statistical learning and pattern-finding, processes of entrenchment of constructions in memory related to frequency and usage effects, capacities for abstraction and schematisation, and sociocognitive capacities such as perspective-taking, ostensive–inferential communication, shared and collective intentionality, the ability to converge on shared conventions, the dynamic, interactive co-creation of meaning in interaction, as well as others. On the other hand, this relates to specifying the processes that lead to the emergence of structure over repeated interactions in communities of practice and over the course of cultural transmission. It is here that cognitive linguistics and usage-based approaches can make significant contributions to language evolution research, as they show how language and structure emerge from interaction and usage. As discussed before, it is especially work on historical language change that can yield insights into processes that have not only led to the emergence of structure in living languages but can also explain the emergence of the first (protolinguistic) constructions both in interactional face-to-face encounters and their increasing conventionalisation and transmission within communities.

Cognitive-linguistic, usage-based approaches on the one hand, and evolutionary linguistics on the other, are highly compatible in their overall conceptualisation of language. Specifically, usage-based approaches (e.g., Beckner et al. 2009) and evolutionary linguistics (e.g., Steels 2011; Kirby 2012) see language as a complex adaptive system. In a complex adaptive system, the global characteristics of the system emerge out of the complex local interactions of different factors in different dimensions and on different timescales. Four timescales are of particular importance in language evolution (cf. Kirby 2012; Hartmann & Pleyer 2021; Pleyer 2023; Enfield 2014, 2022; Sinha 2015):[8]

- The *enchronic timescale* of language use in context and social interaction
- The *ontogenetic timescale* of individual language development across the lifespan
- The *diachronic (or glossogenetic) timescale* of social/cultural historical change
- The *phylogenetic timescale* of bio-cultural language evolution.

For all timescales, cognitive linguistics and usage-based approaches can make important theoretical contributions. For example, regarding the ontogenetic timescale, usage-based accounts of language acquisition have amassed a wealth of relevant research on the cognitive and social-interactive processes

---

[8] Note that there have been slightly different proposals for distinguishing the relevant timescales – for instance, Sinha (2015) distinguishes between phylogenesis, sociogenesis, ontogenesis, and microgenesis, the latter referring to 'collaborative situated learning and development'; Enfield (2014: 7–9) proposed what he calls the MOPEDS model ('Microgenetic-Ontogenetic-Phylogenetic-Enchronic-Diachronic-Synchronic'). Also, the individual timescales can be broken down further – for instance, Larsen-Freeman & Cameron (2008: 169) have proposed a set of 'timescales relevant to face-to-face conversation between two people', e.g., a mental processing timescale, an online talk timescale, and a discourse event timescale (also see Enfield 2014: 12; see Uryu et al. 2014 for discussion). For expository purposes, we will stick with the four timescales mentioned here.

and mechanisms children use to 'construct a language' and acquire a network of constructions (e.g., Tomasello 2003; Ibbotson 2020; see also Section 4).

Concerning the 'to-and-fro of social interaction' (Enfield 2022) that makes up the enchronic timescale, one interesting proposal of how structure emerges in interaction is that of 'ad hoc constructionalization' (Brône & Zima 2014). In ad hoc constructionalisation, local patterns and temporary constructions emerge and can be used as a shared linguistic resource for the duration of the encounter. Du Bois (2014), Pleyer (2017, 2023), and Verhagen (2021) argue that the emergence of such patterns in interaction can serve as the starting point for their increasing recurrence in subsequent interactions, leading to their increasing conventionalisation in a community of practice. This, in turn, as briefly outlined in the model sketch that we will discuss later in this section, then can serve as the foundation for the cumulative cultural evolution of language. As this shows, and as we have seen throughout this Element, a usage-based approach to the diachronic timescale can uncover many of the evolutionary dynamics in language change, as well as shed light on the cognitive and social factors that influence it. One particularly promising model that combines the enchronic, ontogenetic, and diachronic timescales is Schmid's (2020) entrenchment-and-conventionalisation model. This approach models the interaction of the cognitive (entrenchment) and the social (conventionalisation) dimension of language, which are connected in a feedback loop through the driving force of usage. On the cognitive and individual dimension, repeated encounters with a particular structure strengthen its storage and representation in memory. On the community dimension, frequently occurring structures diffuse and become established and socially shared within a community of practice. The interaction and mutual reinforcement of these processes leads to language change. As these processes take domain-general cognitive processes as well as social interaction and usage as its starting points, this approach also has the potential to help explain the emergence of the first entrenched and conventionalised protolinguistic structures. In other words, it can be used as a model for the emergence of language through interaction, entrenchment on the cognitive side, and conventionalisation on the community side (Pleyer 2023). Such an approach takes seriously the fact that language is both a cognitive and a social phenomenon (Dąbrowska 2020), and sees their interaction in usage as a key driving force in language evolution. In doing so, it also takes the interaction between individual and population into account more thoroughly, which has been another focus of recent cognitive-linguistic research (e.g., Petré & Van de Velde 2018; Petré & Anthonissen 2020). As Verhagen (forthcoming) points out, population thinking plays a crucial role in evolution but has arguably often been neglected in linguistic theorising. In particular, he argues that even some recent approaches do not adequately take into account the key insight of population thinking, namely 'that the emergence of conventionality is a community level causal process distinct from the emergence of cognitive units and routines for speaking and understanding' (Verhagen forthcoming). However, some approaches, including the entrenchment-and-conventionalisation model, but also Baxter and Croft's (2016) account of language change across the lifespan or Dąbrowska's (2020) adaptation of Keller's invisible-hand approach, have started to make explicit proposals as to how the relationship between individual and population can be modelled. Also, first attempts have been made to distinguish the levels of individual and population in empirical research. In their analysis of the grammaticalisation of *going to*, for example, Petré & Van de Velde (2018) try to tease apart essentially non-social mechanisms of innovation from inherently social mechanisms of propagation.

Overall, this means that cognitive-linguistic and usage-based approaches can contribute to possible scenarios of language emergence by specifying critical processes and dynamics on the enchronic, ontogenetic, and diachronic timescale. To illustrate this potential, we briefly outline a model of how a cognitive-linguistic, usage-based view of language evolution can capture fundamental processes that have the potential to kick-start language evolution: one foundation for this is the aforementioned 'language-, interaction-, and construction-ready brain'. That is, we take as our starting point basic cognitive and interactional capacities enabling the co-creation of meaning in interactions, and enabling interactants to converge on shared symbolic practices that they could add to open-endedly in repeated interactions. Hominins who first started to develop basic communicative solutions to recurring communication problems would retain those that proved successful. Successful solutions to previous communicative challenges would shape how these challenges were solved in the future (Christiansen & Chater 2022). They would also make it more likely that these communicative strategies were used with different and more and more communicative partners, leading to their social diffusion across a community. Repeated use of these communicative solutions would then lead to these solutions becoming entrenched (on the cognitive side) and conventionalised (on the community side). Over time, usage-based factors would then lead to a repertoire of cognitively entrenched and socially conventionalised (proto) constructions. That is, the first protolinguistic constructions would emerge on the interactional timescale. Through repeated use, they would then become part of a shared community-wide system, becoming entrenched in individuals on the ontogenetic timescale, and be transmitted through the community, and change through the transmission process, on the diachronic timescale. As research on experimental semiotics, IL, and the evolutionary dynamics of language has shown, over time such systems become increasingly more structured and systematic. They also become more abstract and schematic in nature. This process, then, offers a mechanism that can lead to the gradual transition towards the language pole on the protolanguage–language continuum (Hartmann & Pleyer 2021; Pleyer 2023).

Here, cognitive-linguistic models have much to offer for fleshing out such a scenario.

Regarding the phylogenetic timescale, one further interesting contribution of usage-based approaches is a focus on memory processes, and how entrenchment influences linguistic structure. Divjak (2019), for example, outlines three types of entrenchment that influence the mental storage of constructions:

- repeatedly activated structures are processed more rapidly and in a more automated fashion ('What You Do Often, You Do Faster and with Fewer Errors');
- frequently co-occurring structures achieve unit status, and can be retrieved and accessed simultaneously ('Units that Occur Together, Refer Together');
- co-occurring structures fuse together and become chunks ('Units that Occur Together, Blur Together').

This means that structural aspects of language are influenced by the nature of entrenchment in memory. To what degree could these processes also help explain the emergence of structure in protolinguistic hominin communication? This is a question to be further investigated. However, just as an illustration, it can already be brought into dialogue with a specific proposal by Planer and Sterelny (2021) on the emergence of the first composite signs. Planer and Sterelny argue that *Homo erectus* populations (who lived around 1.9 mya to 100 kya[9]) had a basic mixed-modality protolanguage. In this protolanguage, they argue, repair signals would become increasingly frequent. Communicative repair is a pervasive feature in human interaction (e.g., Dingemanse et al. 2015b) and can also be found in the communication of other animals, such as great ape gestural communication (Heesen et al. 2022). As the degree of collaboration and cooperation increased in erectines, for example in the domain of tool-making, this would lead to more repair sequences. In addition, Planer and Sterelny argue that with increased social cognition and 'smartness', interlocutors would anticipate the necessities for repair and integrated repair signals into their initial message. For example, a pointing gesture might at first have been a repair mechanism ('No, this stone'), before becoming part of a composite sign ('Pick up stone' + 'Pointing at stone/This stone'). Although Planer and

---

[9] mya = million years ago; kya = thousand years ago.

Sterelny do not make explicit reference to processes of entrenchment, the process that is described here is captured quite well by the results of entrenchment explicated by Divjak (2019): repeatedly co-occurring items are stored as units, enabling their simultaneous access and retrieval, and repeatedly co-occurring structures become fused and chunked together, becoming a 'referential unit'.

A cognitive-linguistic approach also has the advantage that it can help bridge the gap between questions of language origins and language development. As mentioned at the beginning of this Element, it has sometimes been criticised that the term *language evolution* conflates both aspects. And indeed, it is largely research on the cultural evolution of language that immediately seems highly compatible with the usage-based approach pursued in cognitive linguistics. However, we have also argued that research on the communication systems of non-human animals can partly be understood using concepts from cognitive linguistics. This seems straightforward as cognitive linguistics is interested in the interconnection between language, cognition, and the social and cultural environments in which language use takes place. In addition, it makes sense not to draw a categorical distinction between linguistic and non-linguistic signs but to conceive of language as one semiotic resource among others. This follows out of the gradualist approach of cognitive linguistics, evident in its embracement of prototype theory (e.g., Lakoff 1987) and in concepts like the lexicon-syntax continuum that plays a crucial role in Construction Grammar (Ungerer & Hartmann 2023). This gradualist approach, then, also offers a heuristic framework for modelling the emergence of linguistic signs out of pre-linguistic precursors.

In our discussion of the 'shopping list' approach, we have listed some of the cognitive capacities that needed to evolve for a 'language-, interaction-, and construction-ready brain', but these of course also need to be complemented with references to physiological and anatomical changes supporting the evolution of language (cf. Győri 2021). There have been major biological changes during hominin evolution, which served as the platform to make the evolutionary emergence of language via processes of cumulative cultural evolution possible. One of the most obvious ones is the evolution of human brain size, which began significantly increasing around 2 mya. In absolute terms, with an average weight of about 1,400 g, the human brain is roughly three times bigger than the brains of other great apes. In relative terms, the human brain is also significantly bigger than expected for a primate our size (Verendeev & Sherwood 2018). The human brain also differs in terms of its neuroanatomical architecture and brain organisation, with an expanded prefrontal cortex (Deacon 1998) as well as other parts of the cerebral cortex and significant rewiring of fibre tract connections involved in capacities such as tool-making, social cognition, and language (Sherwood 2019; Ponce De León et al. 2021; Langdon 2022: 336–343). Other changes relevant to language include, for example, the evolution of neuroanatomical structures supporting increased fine-grained sensori-motor coordination, motor control, and sequential learning abilities, which are foundational for both spoken and signed language. There were also changes specifically related to the evolution of speech, such as changes in vocal anatomy (see, e.g., Fitch 2010: 297–337 for a review), as well as increased vocal and breath control (e.g., MacLarnon 2012; Fuchs & Rochet-Capellan 2021) and vocal learning abilities (e.g., Zhang 2017). Some of these would have served as pre-adaptations or enabling conditions that were exapted in the evolution of protolanguage. Others would represent adaptations once protolinguistic communication got off the ground (Fitch 2010; MacLarnon 2012), kick-starting a co-evolutionary feedback loop between (proto)language and the capacities supporting it (cf. Johansson 2021). All these changes likely had a gradual and long evolutionary trajectory in the 1.5 million years since *Homo erectus* (Levinson & Holler 2014; Dediu & Levinson 2018) with important foundations of speech present at least since the last common ancestor between Neanderthals and modern humans 500 kya (Dediu & Levinson 2013). Of course, these changes were not restricted to speech. For example, they also include changes influencing the multimodal nature of human communication, such as anatomical and physiological changes related to the biomechanic foundations and muscle systems involved in co-speech gesture (Pouw & Fuchs 2022). Many changes likely had complex and wide-ranging effects, such as the evolution of the globular braincase characteristic of *Homo sapiens*. This development likely was related to significant changes in developmental programmes, neural organisation, and the genetic regulation underlying them (Boeckx & Benítez-Burraco 2014; Meneganzin et al. 2022).

For any scenario of language evolution and the evolution of human cognition, it is a central question which evolutionary forces drove the biological changes and changes in social organisation supporting these capacities. Many different forces and adaptive scenarios have been proposed as driving factors, with different proposals for changes in the evolutionary niche of hominins which acted as selection pressures for the evolution of the capacities underlying language. Many of them are framed in terms of adaptive solutions to ecological, technological, and social challenges faced by hominins in the course of evolution.

For example, some approaches have pointed to ecological challenges that required novel subsistence strategies. These include, for example, coordinated 'power scavenging', in which the predator responsible for the kill was chased away in a coordinated group effort (Bickerton 2009), or complex coordinated hunting (Tomasello 2014), which necessitated more complex communication. Others in turn have highlighted challenges related to the transmission of technological information, with complex communication as a prerequisite for (teaching the skills involved in) the creation of complex tools (e.g., Morgan et al. 2015; Lombao et al. 2017; though see Shilton 2019).

Regarding sociality as a driver of human evolution, an influential line of reasoning has connected the evolution of language and cognition to selection pressures associated with the increasing demands of navigating complex primate social groups, especially managing the complexities of bigger group sizes (e.g., Dunbar & Shultz 2007) as well as the growing importance of culturally acquired knowledge and skills (e.g., Sterelny 2012; Sinha 2015). Proposals have been made for competitive scenarios – as in the 'Machiaviellian Intelligence Hypothesis', which posits that bigger brains and increased social intelligence evolved in order to manipulate and use others in contexts of social competition (Byrne & Whiten 1988) or scenarios focusing on the role of persuasion in communication in such contexts (e.g., Ferretti & Adornetti 2021). Others have stressed the importance of cooperation in human evolution (e.g., Tomasello 2008; see also Section 4), with conflict management and coordination of cooperation as primary drivers of the evolution of human behaviour (e.g., Lee 2018; Newson & Richerson 2021). Language, in these models, has evolved for the management of interactions in social groups. For example, Dunbar (1996) has proposed that language arose out of a form of vocal social grooming required to maintain bigger group sizes. In a similar vein, Benítez-Burraco and Progovac (2020) have argued that humans have undergone a process of self-domestication in which language evolved for social coordination and the management of aggression. Relatedly, Wacewicz and Żywiczyński (2018) have argued that the evolution of a cooperative, community-wide 'platform of trust' was a fundamental prerequisite for the development of language-like systems in hominins.

Many of these approaches see social complexity, cooperative subsistence activities, and the transmission of changing cultural information as responses to ecological challenges that led to the evolution of specifically hominin ways of living and communicating (Sterelny 2012; Newson & Richerson 2021; Planer & Sterelny 2021). A number of approaches have specifically highlighted the role of climate variation as a driver in the evolution of culture. On this view, the heightened instability of hominin habitats acted as a selective pressure for the evolution of a 'cultural niche' scaffolding the development and acquisition of complex cultural behaviours and skills (cf. Potts 2013). Given the importance of acquiring cultural behaviours and knowledge to adaptively respond to a variable and insecure environment, this placed a special demand on children being able to acquire this knowledge in ontogeny and the reallocation of resources to create a developmental niche representing a suitable learning environment.

These ideas are linked to the framework of 'niche construction', which stresses that organisms can modify their environments in a way that has consequences for their own evolutionary trajectories (and those of other species). This includes not only changes in the physical environment (as, for example, in the case of beavers building dams) but also the social and 'epistemic' environment. Humans, on this view, have created a particular niche enabling high-bandwidth transmission of cultural information and the development of complex skills as well as cumulative cultural evolution (e.g., Sterelny 2012). This resulted in the evolution of an extended period of childhood dependency and longer lifespans, coupled with highly plastic brain development influenced by culture, as well as a change towards 'cooperative breeding', in which children were cared for by multiple caregivers. The coordination of such 'allocare' and the importance of acquiring knowledge during childhood necessitated more complex communication, and generally higher cooperativeness, which then 'unlocked' the cooperative information sharing characteristic of language (e.g., Hrdy 2009; Burkart et al. 2018; Isler & van Schaik 2012). These changes would likely also bring with them adaptations for teaching and heightened sensitivity to ostensive–inferential referential communication (Csibra & Gergeley 2009; Heintz & Scott-Phillips 2023). One aspect of this niche was that it also served as a 'language-ready niche of development', which favoured the development of language in hominins with a 'language-ready brain' (Odling-Smee & Laland 2009; Sinha 2015). Cumulative cultural evolution and the niches supporting it would also co-evolve, with more complex cultural behaviours influencing the social structures in which they developed and vice versa, in a feedback loop (Sterelny 2012; Sinha 2015; see also Section 4). This means that (proto)language itself likely acted as a further selection pressure for the evolution of the cognitive, anatomical, and social structures supporting language.

The proliferation of adaptive scenarios has been criticised in the past for being too unconstrained, giving rise to a high volume of potential 'just-so stories', which sound plausible but do not have enough actual evidence and theoretical motivation to back them up (e.g., Bickerton 2009; Fitch, 2010; Johansson 2021). However, recent scenarios have increasingly made progress in integrating a wealth of evidence and theoretical considerations from different disciplines to strengthen their proposals, and as this Element has shown, cognitive linguistics can make significant contributions to such enterprises.

A promising project that must be mentioned here is the Causal Hypotheses in Evolutionary Linguistics Database (CHIELD; pronounced like 'shield') by

Roberts et al. (2020). They have collected a large set of causal hypotheses proposed in theoretical models of language evolution that have been tested in the literature, especially, but not exclusively, in experimental studies (see Section 5). What makes this resource so valuable is that it allows for making connections between different studies, and exploring various hypotheses and the degree to which they have been substantiated in the literature. Importantly, the causal graph set-up of CHIELD forces researchers to make explicit the assumed causal links between different factors (Roberts 2018).

One thing that should be kept in mind when discussing scenarios of language evolution is that, as noted by Parravicini and Pievani (2019), language considered as a trait is 'a complex mosaic of sub-traits with different phylogenetic stories' (see also Boeckx & Benítez-Burraco 2014). This means that the traits supporting language likely evolved following different trajectories and have different evolutionary histories. Similarly, the evolution of human language and cognition likely also was a process of mosaic evolution instead of a single 'cognitive revolution' (e.g., Berwick & Chomsky 2016) representing a sudden 'crossing of the Rubicon' towards behavioural modernity (cf. Meneganzin & Currie 2022). Neither is it simply captured by a steady and gradual cumulative change towards behavioural modernity (McBrearty & Brooks 2000). Instead, the mosaic evolution of behavioural modernity, including language, likely represents a long, protracted, historically contingent process with fits and starts, and interchanging periods of stasis and innovation. It was highly reliant on cultural, contextual, and demographic conditions, which likely took a long time to stabilise and lead to the social environments required to support high-fidelity cumulative cultural evolution of cognitively modern behaviours, including language (Meneganzin & Currie 2022; Scerri & Will 2023).

As this Element has shown, cognitive linguistics as a framework is ideally suited to help in understanding both the mosaic nature of the structures supporting language as well as their mosaic evolution.

References

Aitchison, Jean. 2008. *The articulate mammal: An introduction to psycholinguistics*. 5th ed. York: Routledge.

Akhtar, Nameera, Malinda Carpenter & Michael Tomasello. 1996. The role of discourse novelty in early word learning. *Child Development* 67. 635–645. https://doi.org/10.1111/j.1467-8624.1996.tb01756.x.

Amphaeris, Jenny, Graeme Shannon & Thora Tenbrink. 2021. Cognitive linguistics support for the evolution of language from animal cognition. *Proceedings of the Annual Meeting of the Cognitive Science Society* 43-(43).2609–2615. https://escholarship.org/uc/item/46s8778g.

Amphaeris, Jenny, Graeme Shannon & Thora Tenbrink. 2022. Overlap not gap: Understanding the relationship between animal communication and language with prototype theory. *Lingua* 272. 103332. https://doi.org/10.1016/j.lingua.2022.103332.

Anderson, Stephen R. 2004. *Doctor Dolittle's delusion: Animals and the uniqueness of human language*. New Haven, CT: Yale University Press.

Arbib, Michael A. 2012. *How the brain got language: The mirror systems hypothesis*. Oxford: Oxford University Press.

Armstrong, David F. & Sherman E. Wilcox (eds.). 2007. *The gestural origin of language*. Oxford: Oxford University Press.

Astington, Janet W. & Jodie A. Baird (eds.). 2005. *Why language matters for theory of mind*. Oxford: Oxford University Press.

Azevedo, Frederico A. C., Ludmila R. B. Carvalho, Lea T. Grinberg et al. 2009. Equal numbers of neuronal and nonneuronal cells make the human brain an isometrically scaled-up primate brain. *Journal of Comparative Neurology* 513(5). 532–541. https://doi.org/10.1002/cne.21974.

Baldwin, Dare A. 1993. Infants' ability to consult the speaker for clues to word reference. *Journal of Child Language* 20. 395–418. https://doi.org/10.1017/S0305000900008345.

Baldwin, Dare A. & Louis J. Moses. 2001. Links between social understanding and early word learning: Challenges to current accounts. *Social Development* 10. 309–329. https://doi.org/10.1111/1467-9507.00168.

Bartlett, Frederic C. 1932. *Remembering: A study in experimental and social psychology*. Cambridge: Cambridge University Press.

Bauer, Laurie, Rochelle Lieber & Ingo Plag. 2013. *The Oxford reference guide to English morphology*. Oxford: Oxford University Press.

Bavelas, Alex. 1952. Communication patterns in problem-solving groups. In Heinz von Foerster (ed.), *Cybernetics. Circular, causal and feedback mechanisms in biological and social systems: Transactions of the ninth conference*, 1–44. New York: Josiah Macy Jr. Foundation.

Baxter, Gareth & William Croft. 2016. Modeling language change across the lifespan: Individual trajectories in community change. *Language Variation and Change* 28(2). 129–173. https://doi.org/10.1017/S0954394516000077.

Beckner, Clay, Richard Blythe, Joan Bybee et al. 2009. Language is a complex adaptive system: Position paper. *Language Learning* 59(Suppl. 1). 1–26. https://doi.org/10.1111/j.1467-9922.2009.00533.x.

Behne, Tanya, Malinda Carpenter & Michael Tomasello. 2005. One-year-olds comprehend the communicative intentions behind gestures in a hiding game. *Developmental Science* 8. 492–499. https://doi.org/10.1111/j.1467-7687.2005.00440.x.

Benítez-Burraco, Antonio & Ljiljana Progovac. 2020. A four-stage model for language evolution under the effects of human self-domestication. *Language & Communication* 73. 1–17. https://doi.org/10.1016/j.langcom.2020.03.002.

Benítez-Burraco, Antonio & Ljiljana Progovac. 2021. Reconstructing prehistoric languages. *Philosophical Transactions of the Royal Society B: Biological Sciences* 376(1824). https://doi.org/10.1098/rstb.2020.0187.

Bergmann, Till & Rick Dale. 2016. A sociometric analysis of Evolang: Intersections and authorships. In Seán G. Roberts, Christine Cuskley, Luke McCrohon et al. (eds.), *The evolution of language: Proceedings of the 11th International Conference*, 79–86. http://evolang.org/neworleans/papers/185.html.

Berwick, Robert C. & Noam Chomsky. 2016. *Why only us: Language and evolution*. Cambridge, MA: MIT Press.

Bettle, Rosemary & Alexandra G. Rosati. 2021. The primate origins of human social cognition. *Language Learning and Development* 17(2). 96–127. www.tandfonline.com/doi/abs/10.1080/15475441.2020.1820339.

Bickerton, Derek. 1990. *Language and species*. Chicago: University of Chicago Press.

Bickerton, Derek. 2009. *Adam's tongue: How humans made language, how language made humans*. New York: Hill and Wang.

Boeckx, Cedric & Antonio Benítez-Burraco. 2014. Globularity and language-readiness: Generating new predictions by expanding the set of genes of interest. *Frontiers in Psychology* 5. 1324. https://doi.org/10.3389/fpsyg.2014.01324.

Bohn, Manuel, Josep Call & Michael Tomasello. 2015. Communication about absent entities in great apes and human infants. *Cognition* 145. 63–72. https://doi.org/10.1016/j.cognition.2015.08.009.

Burkart, Judith, Eloisa Guerreiro Martins, Fabia Miss & Yvonne Zürcher. 2018. From sharing food to sharing information: Cooperative breeding and language evolution. *Interaction Studies* 19(1–2). 136–150. https://doi.org/10.1075/is.17026.bur.

Bradbury, Jack W. & Sandra Lee Vehrencamp. 2011. *Principles of animal communication*. 2nd ed. Sunderland, MA: Sinauer Associates.

Braithwaite, Ben. 2020. Ideologies of linguistic research on small sign languages in the global South: A Caribbean perspective. *Language & Communication* 74. 182–194. https://doi.org/10.1016/j.langcom.2020.06.009.

Brentari, Diane & Marie Coppola. 2013. What sign language creation teaches us about language. *WIREs Cognitive Science* 4(2). 201–211. https://doi.org/10.1002/wcs.1212.

Brône, Geert & Elisabeth Zima. 2014. Towards a dialogic construction grammar: Ad hoc routines and resonance activation. *Cognitive Linguistics* 25(3). 457–495. https://doi.org/10.1515/cog-2014-0027.

Brysbaert, Marc, Michaël Stevens, Paweł Mandera & Emmanuel Keuleers. 2016. How many words do we know? Practical estimates of vocabulary size dependent on word definition, the degree of language input and the participant's age. *Frontiers in Psychology* 7. www.frontiersin.org/articles/10.3389/fpsyg.2016.01116.

Bybee, Joan L. 2010. *Language, usage and cognition*. Cambridge: Cambridge University Press.

Byrne, Richard & Andrew Whiten (eds.). 1988. *Machiavellian intelligence: Social expertise and the evolution of intellect in monkeys, apes and humans*. Oxford: Oxford University Press.

Byrne, Richard W, Erica Cartmill, Emilie Genty et al. 2017. Great ape gestures: Intentional communication with a rich set of innate signals. *Animal Cognition* 20(4). 755–769. https://link.springer.com/article/10.1007/s10071-017-1127-1

Call, Josep & Michael Tomasello. 2008. Does the chimpanzee have a theory of mind? Thirty years later. *Trends in Cognitive Sciences* 12. 187–192. www.sciencedirect.com/science/article/abs/pii/S1364661308000892.

Campbell, Lyle. 2013. *Historical linguistics: An introduction*. 3rd ed. Cambridge, MA: MIT Press.

Cappelle, Bert. 2006. Particle placement and the case for 'allostructions'. *Constructions* 7(SI1). www.constructions-online.de. https://doi.org/10.24338/CONS-381.

Cartmill, Erica A. & Catherine Hobaiter. 2019. Developmental perspectives on primate gesture: 100 years in the making. *Animal Cognition* 22. 453–459. https://doi.org/10.1007/s10071-019-01279-w.

Catchpole, Clive K. & Peter J. B. Slater. 2008. *Bird song: Biological themes and variations*. 2nd ed. Cambridge: Cambridge University Press.

Cheney, Dorothy L. & Robert M. Seyfarth. 1990. *How monkeys see the world: Inside the mind of another species*. Chicago: University of Chicago Press.

Christiansen, Morten H. & Nick Chater. 2022. *The language game: How improvisation created language and changed the world*. London: Penguin Press.

Crockford, Catherine, Roman M. Wittig & Klaus Zuberbühler. 2017. Vocalizing in chimpanzees is influenced by social-cognitive processes. *Science Advances* 3(11). e1701742. https://doi.org/10.1126/sciadv.1701742.

Croft, William. 2000. *Explaining language change: An evolutionary approach*. Harlow: Pearson Longman.

Creanza, Nicole, Oren Kolodny & Marcus W. Feldman. 2017. Cultural evolutionary theory: How culture evolves and why it matters. *Proceedings of the National Academy of Sciences* 114(30). 7782–7789. https://doi.org/10.1073/pnas.1620732114.

Csibra, Gergely & György Gergely. 2009. Natural pedagogy. *Trends in Cognitive Sciences* 13(4). 148–153. https://doi.org/10.1016/j.tics.2009.01.005.

Dąbrowska, Ewa. 2020. Language as a phenomenon of the third kind. *Cognitive Linguistics* 31(2), 213–229. https://doi.org/10.1515/cog-2019-0029.

Dawkins, Richard. 2006. *The selfish gene*. 3rd ed. Oxford: Oxford University Press.

De Vos, Connie & Roland Pfau. 2015. Sign language typology: The contribution of rural sign languages. *Annual Review of Linguistics* 1. 265–288. www.annualreviews.org/doi/abs/10.1146/annurev-linguist-030514-124958.

De Waal, Frans. 2016. *Are we smart enough to know how smart animals are?* New York: WW Norton.

Deacon, Terrence W. 1998. *The symbolic species: The co-evolution of language and the brain*. New York: W. W. Norton.

Dediu, Dan & Stephen C. Levinson. 2013. On the antiquity of language: The reinterpretation of Neandertal linguistic capacities and its consequences. *Frontiers in Psychology* 4. 397. https://doi.org/10.3389/fpsyg.2013.00397.

Dediu, Dan & Stephen C. Levinson. 2018. Neanderthal language revisited: Not only us. *Current Opinion in Behavioral Sciences* 21. 49–55. https://doi.org/10.1016/j.cobeha.2018.01.001.

De Smet, Hendrik, Frauke D'hoedt, Lauren Fonteyn & Kristel Van Goethem. 2018. The changing functions of competing forms: Attraction and differentiation. *Cognitive Linguistics* 29(2). 197–234. www.degruyter.com/document/doi/10.1515/cog-2016-0025/html?lang=en

DeGraff, Michel. 2003. Against creole exceptionalism. *Language* 79(2). 391–410. www.jstor.org/stable/4489423.

DeGraff, Michel. 2005. Linguists' most dangerous myth: The fallacy of Creole Exceptionalism. *Language in Society* 34(4).533–591. https://doi.org/10.1017/S0047404505050207.

Delliponti, Angelo, Renato Raia, Giulia Sanguedolce et al. 2023. Experimental semiotics: A systematic categorization of experimental studies on the bootstrapping of communication systems. *Biosemiotics* 16. 291–310. https://doi.org/10.1007/s12304-023-09534-x.

Deshpande, Adwait, Erica van de Waal & Klaus Zuberbühler. 2023. Context-dependent alarm responses in wild vervet monkeys. *Animal Cognition* 26. 1199–1208. https://doi.org/10.1007/s10071-023-01767-0.

Dingemanse, Mark, Damián E. Blasi, Gary Lupyan, Morten H. Christiansen & Padraic Monaghan. 2015a. Arbitrariness, iconicity, and systematicity in language. *Trends in Cognitive Sciences* 19(10). 603–615. https://doi.org/10.1016/j.tics.2015.07.013.

Dingemanse, Mark, Seán G. Roberts, Julija Baranova et al. 2015b. Universal principles in the repair of communication problems. *PloS One* 10(9). e0136100. https://doi.org/10.1371/journal.pone.0136100.

Divjak, Dagmar. 2019. *Frequency in language: Memory, attention and learning*. Cambridge: Cambridge University Press.

Dong, Shihao, Tao Lin, James C. Nieh & Ken Tan. 2023. Social signal learning of the waggle dance in honey bees. *Science* 379(6636). 1015–1018. https://doi.org/10.1126/science.ade1702.

Du Bois, John W. 2014. Towards a dialogic syntax. *Cognitive Linguistics* 25(3). 359–410. https://doi.org/10.1515/cog-2014-0024.

Dunbar, Robin I. M. 1996. *Grooming, gossip, and the evolution of language*. Harvard: Harvard University Press.

Dunbar, Robin I. M. & Susanne Shultz. 2007. Evolution in the social brain. *Science* 317(5843). 1344–1347. https://doi.org/10.1126/science.1145463.

Enfield, Nick J. 2014. *Natural causes of language: Frames, biases and cultural transmission* (Conceptual Foundations of Language Science 1). Berlin: Language Science Press.

Enfield, Nick J. 2022. Enchrony. *Wiley Interdisciplinary Reviews: Cognitive Science* 13(4). e1597. https://doi.org/10.1002/wcs.1597.

Engelmann, Jan M., Esther Herrmann & Michael Tomasello. 2012. Five-year olds, but not chimpanzees, attempt to manage their reputations. *PLoS One*. Public Library of Science San Francisco, USA 7(10). e48433. https://jour nals.plos.org/plosone/article?id=10.1371/journal.pone.0048433.

Engesser, Sabrina & Simon W Townsend. 2019. Combinatoriality in the vocal systems of nonhuman animals. *Wiley Interdisciplinary Reviews: Cognitive Science* 10(4). e1493. https://doi.org/10.1002/wcs.1493.

Engesser, Sabrina, Jennifer L. Holub, Louis G. O'Neill, Andrew F. Russell & Simon W. Townsend. 2019. Chestnut-crowned babbler calls are composed of meaningless shared building blocks. *Proceedings of the National Academy of Sciences* 116(39). 19579–19584. https://doi.org/10.1073/pnas.1819513116.

Esper, Erwin Allen. 1925. *A technique for the experimental investigation of associative interference in artificial linguistic material*. Philadelphia: Linguistic Society of America.

Evans, Vyvyan & Melanie Green. 2006. *Cognitive linguistics: An Introduction*. Edinburgh: Edinburgh University Press.

Everett, Caleb. 2013. *Linguistic relativity: Evidence across languages and cognitive domains* (Applications of Cognitive Linguistics 25). Berlin: De Gruyter Mouton.

Fauconnier, Gilles. 2004. Pragmatics and cognitive linguistics. In Laurence R. Horn & Gregory Ward (eds.), *Handbook of pragmatics*, 657–674. Malden, MA: Wiley-Blackwell.

Fauconnier, Gilles & Mark Turner. 2002. *The way we think: Conceptual blending and the mind's hidden complexities*. New York: Basic Books.

Fay, Nicolas, Casey J. Lister, T. Mark Ellison & Susan Goldin-Meadow. 2014. Creating a communication system from scratch: Gesture beats vocalization hands down. *Frontiers in Psychology* 5. www.frontiersin.org/articles/ 10.3389/fpsyg.2014.00354.

Fedzechkina, Masha, Lucy Hall Hartley & Gareth Roberts. 2023. Social biases can lead to less communicatively efficient languages. *Language Acquisition* 30(3–4). 230–255. https://doi.org/10.1080/10489223.2022.2057229.

Fenson, Larry, Philip S. Dale, J. Steven Reznick & Elizabeth Bates. 1994. Variability in early communicative development. *Monographs of the Society for Research in Child Development* 59(5). 1–173. www.jstor.org/ stable/1166093.

Ferretti, Francesco & Ines Adornetti. 2021. Persuasive conversation as a new form of communication in Homo sapiens. *Philosophical Transactions of the Royal Society B* 376(1824). 20200196. https://doi.org/10.1098/ rstb.2020.0196.

Fichtel, Claudia & Peter M. Kappeler. 2011. Variation in the meaning of alarm calls in Verreaux's and Coquerel's Sifakas (Propithecus verreauxi, P. coquereli). *International Journal of Primatology* 32(2). 346–361. https://doi.org/10.1007/s10764-010-9472-9.

Fischer, Julia. 2017. Primate vocal production and the riddle of language evolution. *Psychonomic Bulletin & Review* 24(1). 72–78. https://doi.org/10.3758/s13423-016-1076-8.

Fischer, Julia, Franziska Wegdell, Franziska Trede, Federica Dal Pesco & Kurt Hammerschmidt. 2020. Vocal convergence in a multi-level primate society: Insights into the evolution of vocal learning. *Proceedings of the Royal Society B: Biological Sciences* 287(1941). 20202531. https://doi.org/10.1098/rspb.2020.2531.

Fitch, W. Tecumseh. 2010. *The evolution of language*. Cambridge: Cambridge University Press.

Fitch, W. Tecumseh. 2018. Bio-Linguistics: Monkeys break through the syntax barrier. *Current Biology* 28(12). R695–R697. https://doi.org/10.1016/j.cub.2018.04.087.

Fitch, W. Tecumseh, Bart de Boer, Neil Mathur & Asif A. Ghazanfar. 2016. Monkey vocal tracts are speech-ready. *Science Advances* 2(12). e1600723. https://doi.org/10.1126/sciadv.1600723.

Flom, Ross & Sarah Johnson. 2011. The effects of adults' affective expression and direction of visual gaze on 12-month-olds' visual preferences for an object following a 5-minute, 1-day, or 1-month delay. *British Journal of Developmental Psychology* 29. 64–85. https://doi.org/10.1348/026151010x512088.

Flower, Tom. 2022. Deception in animal communication. In Todd M. Freeberg, Amanda R. Ridley & Patrizia d'Ettore (eds.), *The Routledge international handbook of comparative psychology*, 274–288. New York: Routledge.

Fouts, Roger & Stepen Tukel Mills. 1998. *Next of kin: My conversations with chimpanzees*. New York: Harper.

Fouts, Roger S. & Deborah H. Fouts. 1989. Loulis in conversation with the cross-fostered chimpanzees. In R. Allen Gardner, Beatrice T. Gardner & Thomas E. Van Cantfort (eds.), *Teaching sign language to chimpanzees*, 293–307. Albany: State University of New York Press.

Freeberg, Todd M., D. L. Book, Hwayoung Jung & Steven C. Kyle. 2021. Communication, cues, and signals. In Todd K. Shackelford & Viviana A. Weekes-Shackelford (eds.), *Encyclopedia of evolutionary psychological science*, 1206–1214. Cham: Springer International. https://doi.org/10.1007/978-3-319-19650-3_2728.

Frisch, Karl von. 1967. *The dance language and orientation of bees.* Cambridge, MA: Harvard University Press.

Fuchs, Susanne & Amélie Rochet-Capellan. 2021. The respiratory foundations of spoken language. *Annual Review of Linguistics* 7. 13–30. https://doi.org/10.1146/annurev-linguistics-031720-103907.

Galantucci, Bruno. 2005. An experimental study of the emergence of human communication systems. *Cognitive Science* 29(5). 737–767. https://doi.org/10.1207/s15516709cog0000/_34.

Galantucci, Bruno. 2017. Experimental semiotics. In Mark Aronoff (ed.), *Oxford research encyclopedia of linguistics.* Oxford: Oxford University Press. https://doi.org/10.1093/acrefore/9780199384655.013.210.

Galantucci, Bruno, Simon Garrod & Gareth Roberts. 2012. Experimental semiotics. *Language and Linguistics Compass* 6(8). 477–493. https://doi.org/10.1002/lnc3.351.

Gardner, R. Allen & Beatrice T. Gardner. 1969. Teaching sign language to a chimpanzee. *Science* 165(3894). 664–672. www.jstor.org/stable/1727877.

Garrod, Simon & Anthony Anderson. 1987. Saying what you mean in dialogue: A study in conceptual and semantic co-ordination. *Cognition* 27(2). 181–218. https://doi.org/10.1016/0010-0277(87)90018-7.

Garrod, Simon & Gwyneth Doherty. 1994. Conversation, co-ordination and convention: An empirical investigation of how groups establish linguistic conventions. *Cognition* 53(3). 181–215. https://doi.org/10.1016/0010-0277(94)90048-5.

Garrod, Simon, Nicolas Fay, John Lee, Jon Oberlander & Tracy MacLeod. 2007. Foundations of representation: Where might graphical symbol systems come from? *Cognitive Science* 31(6). 961–987. https://doi.org/10.1080/03640210701703659.

Geeraerts, Dirk. 2006. Introduction: A rough guide to cognitive linguistics. In Dirk Geeraerts (ed.), *Cognitive linguistics: Basic readings*, 1–28. Berlin: De Gruyter.

Genty, Emilie & Klaus Zuberbühler. 2015. Iconic gesturing in bonobos. *Communicative & Integrative Biology* 8(1). e992742. www.tandfonline.com/doi/full/10.4161/19420889.2014.992742.

Gill, Sharon A. & Andrea M.-K. Bierema. 2013. On the meaning of alarm calls: A review of functional reference in avian alarm calling. *Ethology* 119(6). 449–461. https://doi.org/10.1111/eth.12097.

Giurfa, Martin. 2021. Learning of sameness/difference relationships by honey bees: Performance, strategies and ecological context. *Current Opinion in Behavioral Sciences* (Same-Different Conceptualization) 37. 1–6. https://doi.org/10.1016/j.cobeha.2020.05.008.

Goldberg, Adele E. 1995. *Constructions: A construction grammar approach to argument structure.* Chicago: The University of Chicago Press.

Gong, Tao, Lan Shuai & Bernard Comrie. 2014. Evolutionary linguistics: Theory of language in an interdisciplinary space. *Language Sciences* 41. 243–253. https://doi.org/10.1016/j.langsci.2013.05.001.

Gumperz, John J. & Stephen C. Levinson (eds.). 1996. *Rethinking linguistic relativity.* Cambridge: Cambridge University Press.

Guzmán Naranjo, Matías & Olivier Bonami. 2023. A distributional assessment of rivalry in word formation. *Word Structure* 16(1). 87–114. www.euppubl ishing.com/doi/abs/10.3366/word.2023.0222.

Győri, Gábor. 2021. Cognitive linguistics and language evolution. In Xu Wen & John R. Taylor (eds.), *The Routledge handbook of cognitive linguistics* (Routledge Handbooks in Linguistics), 643–661. New York: Routledge.

Harder, Peter. 2010. *Meaning in mind and society: A functional contribution to the social turn in cognitive linguistics.* Berlin: De Gruyter Mouton.

Hare, Brian & Michael Tomasello. 2004. Chimpanzees are more skillful in competitive than in co-operative cognitive tasks. *Animal Behaviour* 68. 571–581. www.sciencedirect.com/science/article/abs/pii/S00033472040 01678.

Harnad, Stevan. 1990. The symbol grounding problem. *Physica D: Nonlinear Phenomena* 42(1). 335–346. https://doi.org/10.1016/0167-2789(90) 90087-6.

Hartmann, Stefan & Michael Pleyer. 2021. Constructing a protolanguage: Reconstructing prehistoric languages in a usage-based construction grammar framework. *Philosophical Transactions of the Royal Society B: Biological Sciences* 376(1824). https://doi.org/10.1098/rstb.2020.0200.

Haspelmath, Martin. 1999. Why is grammaticalization irreversible? *Linguistics* 37(6). 1043–1068. https://doi.org/10.1515/ling.37.6.1043.

Haspelmath, Martin. 2016. The evolution (or diachrony) of 'language evolution'. Billet. *Diversity Linguistics Comment.* https://dlc.hypotheses.org/894. (9 February 2023).

Hauser, Marc D. 1996. *The evolution of communication.* Cambridge, MA: MIT Press.

Hayes, Keith J. & Catherine Hayes. 1951. The intellectual development of a home-raised chimpanzee. *Proceedings of the American Philosophical Society* 95(2). 105–109. www.jstor.org/stable/3143327.

Heesen, Raphaela, Marlen Fröhlich, Christine Sievers, Marieke Woensdregt & Mark Dingemanse. 2022. Coordinating social action: A primer for the cross-species investigation of communicative repair. *Philosophical*

Transactions of the Royal Society of London B: Biological Sciences 377-(1859). 20210110. https://doi.org/10.1098/rstb.2021.0110.

Heine, Bernd & Tania Kuteva. 2007. *The genesis of grammar: A reconstruction.* Oxford: Oxford University Press.

Heintz, Christophe & Thom Scott-Phillips. 2023. Expression unleashed: The evolutionary and cognitive foundations of human communication. *Behavioral and Brain Sciences* 46. e1. https://doi.org/10.1017/S0140525 X22000012.

Henner, Jon & Octavian Robinson. 2023. Unsettling languages, unruly body-minds: A crip linguistics manifesto. *Journal of Critical Study of Communication & Disability* 1(1). 7–37. https://doi.org/10.48516/jcscd_2023 vol1iss1.4.

Herrmann, Esther & Michael Tomasello. 2006. Apes' and children's under-standing of cooperative and competitive motives in a communicative situ-ation. *Developmental Science* 9. 518–529. https://onlinelibrary.wiley.com/doi/abs/10.1111/j.1467-7687.2006.00519.x.

Heyes, Cecilia & Richard Moore. 2023. Henrich, Heyes, and Tomasello on the cognitive foundations of cultural evolution. In Jamshid J. Tehrani, Jeremy Kendal & Rachel Kendal (eds.), *The Oxford handbook of cultural evolution.* Oxford: Oxford University Press. https://doi.org/10.1093/oxfordhb/9780198869252.013.17.

Hobaiter, Catherine, Kirsty E. Graham & Richard W. Byrne. 2022. Are ape gestures like words? Outstanding issues in detecting similarities and differ-ences between human language and ape gesture. *Philosophical Transactions of the Royal Society B: Biological Sciences* 377(1860). 20210301. https://doi.org/10.1098/rstb.2021.0301.

Hockett, Charles F. 1959. Animal 'languages' and human language. In J. N. Spuhler (ed.), *The evolution of man's capacity for culture*, 32–39. Detroit: Wayne State University Press.

Hockett, Charles F. 1960. The origins of speech. *Scientific American* 203. 88–96.

Hockett, Charles F. 1963. The problem of universals in language. In Joseph H. Greenberg (ed.), *Universals of language,* 1–22. Cambridge, MA: MIT Press.

Hockett, Charles F. & Stuart A. Altmann. 1968. A note on design features. In Thomas A. Sebeok (ed.), *Animal communication: Techniques of study and results of research*, 61–72. Bloomington: Indiana University Press.

Hoffmann, Thomas. 2022. *Construction grammar: The structure of English.* Cambridge: Cambridge University Press.

Hopper, Paul J. & Elizabeth Closs Traugott. 2003. *Grammaticalization*. 2nd ed. Cambridge: Cambridge University Press.

Hou, Lynn. 2020. Who signs? Language ideologies about deaf and hearing child signers in one family in Mexico. *Sign Language Studies* 20(4). 664–690. https://doi.org/10.1353/sls.2020.0023.

Hou, Lynn & Connie de Vos. 2022. Classifications and typologies: Labeling sign languages and signing communities. *Journal of Sociolinguistics* 26(1). 118–125. https://doi.org/10.1111/josl.12490.

Hrdy, Sarah Blaffer (2009). *Mothers and others: The evolutionary origins of mutual understanding*. Cambridge, MA: Harvard University Press.

Hu, Jane C. 2014. Koko, Kanzi, and ape language research: Criticism of working conditions and animal care. https://slate.com/technology/2014/08/koko-kanzi-and-ape-language-research-criticism-of-working-conditions-and-animal-care.html.

Hull, David L. 1988. *Science as a process: An evolutionary account of the social and conceptual development of science*. Chicago: University of Chicago Press.

Hurford, James R. 2007. *The origins of meaning: Language in the light of evolution, Vol. 1*. Oxford: Oxford University Press.

Hurford, James R. 2012. *The origins of grammar: Language in the light of evolution, Vol. 2* (Oxford Studies in the Evolution of Language). Oxford: Oxford University Press.

Ibbotson, Paul. 2020. *What it takes to talk: Exploring developmental cognitive linguistics* (Cognitive Linguistics Research 64). Berlin: De Gruyter.

Isler, Karin & van Schaik, Carel P. 2012. Allomaternal care, life history and brain size evolution in mammals. *Journal of Human Evolution* 63(1). 52–63. https://doi.org/10.1016/j.jhevol.2012.03.009.

Ito, Chiyuki & Naomi H. Feldman. 2022. Iterated learning models of language change: A Case study of Sino-Korean accent. *Cognitive Science* 46(4). e13115. https://doi.org/10.1111/cogs.13115.

Jackendoff, Ray. 2010. Your theory of language evolution depends on your theory of language. In Hiroko Yamakido, Richard K. Larson & Viviane Déprez (eds.), *The evolution of human language: Biolinguistic perspectives* (Approaches to the Evolution of Language), 63–72. Cambridge: Cambridge University Press.

Jiang, Xinjian, Tenghai Long, Weicong Cao et al. 2018. Production of supra-regular spatial sequences by macaque monkeys. *Current Biology* 28(12). 1851–1859.e4. https://doi.org/10.1016/j.cub.2018.04.047.

Johansson, Sverker. 2016. Protolanguage possibilities in a construction grammar framework. In Sean G. Roberts, Christine Cuskley, Luke McCrohon et al. (eds.), *The evolution of language: Proceedings of the 11th International Conference on the Evolution of Language* (EVOLANG 11). New Orleans. https://evolang.org/neworleans/pdf/EVOLANG_11_paper_149.pdf.

Johansson, Sverker. 2021. *The dawn of language: The story of how we came to talk*. (Trans. Frank Perry). London: MacLehose Press.

Kaminski, Juliane, Josep Call & Julia Fischer. 2004. Word learning in a domestic dog: Evidence for 'fast mapping'. *Science*. 304(5677). 1682–1683. https://doi.org/10.1126/science.1097859.

Kano, Fumihiro, Christopher Krupenye, Satoshi Hirata, Masaki Tomonaga & Josep Call. 2019. Great apes use self-experience to anticipate an agent's action in a false-belief test. *Proceedings of the National Academy of Sciences* 116(42). 20904–20909. https://doi.org/10.1073/pnas.1910095116.

Kaplan, Abby. 2016. *Women talk more than men … And other myths about language explained*. Cambridge: Cambridge University Press.

Keller, Rudi. 1994. *Sprachwandel: Von der unsichtbaren Hand in der Sprache*. 2nd ed. Tübingen: Francke.

Kempe, Vera, Nicolas Gauvrit & Douglas Forsyth. 2015. Structure emerges faster during cultural transmission in children than in adults. *Cognition* 136. 247–254. https://doi.org/10.1016/j.cognition.2014.11.038.

Kempe, Vera, Nicolas Gauvrit, Alison Gibson & Margaret Jamieson. 2019. Adults are more efficient in creating and transmitting novel signalling systems than children. *Journal of Language Evolution* 4(1). 44–70. https://doi.org/10.1093/jole/lzy012.

Kirby, Simon. 2001. Spontaneous evolution of linguistic structure-an iterated learning model of the emergence of regularity and irregularity. *IEEE Transactions on Evolutionary Computation* 5(2). 102–110. https://doi.org/10.1109/4235.918430.

Kirby, Simon. 2012. Language is an adaptive system: The role of cultural evolution in the origins of structure. In Maggie Tallerman & Kathleen R. Gibson (eds.), *The Oxford handbook of language evolution*, 589–604. Oxford: Oxford University Press.

Kirby, Simon, Hannah Cornish & Kenny Smith. 2008. Cumulative cultural evolution in the laboratory: An experimental approach to the origins of structure in human language. *Proceedings of the National Academy of Sciences of the United States of America* 105(31). 10681–10686. https://doi.org/10.1073/pnas.0707835105.

Kirby, Simon, Monica Tamariz, Hannah Cornish & Kenny Smith. 2015. Compression and communication in the cultural evolution of linguistic structure. *Cognition* 141. 87–102. https://doi.org/10.1016/j.cognition.2015.03.016.

Krause, Johannes. 2017. Animal communication. *Oxford Bibliographies*. https://doi.org/10.1093/OBO/9780199772810-0149. (22 May 2023).

Lakoff, George. 1987. *Women, fire, and dangerous things: What categories reveal about the mind.* Chicago: The University of Chicago Press.

Lakoff, George. 1990. The invariance hypothesis: Is abstract reason based on image-schemas? *Cognitive Linguistics* 1. 39–74. https://doi.org/10.1515/cogl.1990.1.1.39.

Lakoff, George & Mark Johnson. 1980. *Metaphors we live by.* Chicago: University of Chicago Press.

Langacker, Ronald W. 2008. *Cognitive grammar: A basic introduction.* Oxford: Oxford University Press.

Langdon, John H. 2022. *Human evolution: Bones, cultures, and genes.* Cham: Springer.

Larsen-Freeman, Diane & Lynne Cameron. 2008. *Complex systems and applied linguistics.* Oxford: Oxford University Press.

Lass, Roger. 1990. How to do things with junk: Exaptation in language evolution. *Journal of Linguistics* 26(1). 79–102. https://doi.org/10.1017/S0022226700014432.

Lass, Roger. 1994. *Old English: A historical linguistic companion.* Cambridge: Cambridge University Press.

Leavens, David A., Timothy P. Racine & William D. Hopkins. 2009. The ontogeny and ohylogeny of non-verbal deixis. In Rudolf Botha & Chris Knight (eds.), *The prehistory of language,* 142–166. Oxford: Oxford University Press.

Lee, Richard B. 2018. Hunter-gatherers and human evolution: New light on old debates. *Annual Review of Anthropology* 47. 513–531. https://doi.org/10.1146/annurev-anthro-102116-041448.

Leeuwen, Edwin J. C. van & William Hoppitt. 2023. Biased cultural transmission of a social custom in chimpanzees. *Science Advances* 9(7). eade5675. https://doi.org/10.1126/sciadv.ade5675.

Lehmann, Christian. 2015. *Thoughts on grammaticalization* (Classics in Linguistics 1). 3rd ed. Berlin: Language Science Press.

Leroux, Maël, Anne M. Schel, Claudia Wilke et al. 2023. Call combinations and compositional processing in wild chimpanzees. *Nature Communications* 14(1). 2225. https://doi.org/10.1038/s41467-023-37816-y.

Levinson, Stephen C. 2003. *Space in language and cognition: Explorations in cognitive diversity.* Cambridge: Cambridge University Press.

Levinson, Stephen C. 2016. Turn-taking in human communication: Origins and implications for language processing. *Trends in Cognitive Sciences* 20(1). 6–14. https://doi.org/10.1016/j.tics.2015.10.010.

Levinson, Stephen C. & Judith Holler. 2014. The origin of human multi-modal communication. *Philosophical Transactions of the Royal Society B: Biological Sciences* 369(1651). 20130302. https://doi.org/10.1098/rstb.2013.0302.

Levshina, Natalia. 2018. Linguistic Frankenstein, or how to test universal constraints without real languages. In Karsten Schmidtke-Bode, Natalia Levshina, Susanne Maria Michaelis & Ilja A. Seržant (eds.), *Explanation in typology: Diachronic sources, functional motivations and the nature of the evidence*, 203–221. Berlin: Language Science Press.

Lewens, Tim & Andrew Buskell. 2023. Cultural evolution. In Edward N. Zalta & Uri Nodelman (eds.), *The Stanford encyclopedia of philosophy*. https://plato.stanford.edu/archives/sum2023/entries/evolution-cultural/. (30 May 2023).

Liebal, Katja, Bridget M. Waller, Katie E. Slocombe & Anne M. Burrows. 2014. *Primate communication: A multimodal approach*. Cambridge: Cambridge University Press.

Liebal, Kristin, Tanya Behne, Malinda Carpenter & Michael Tomasello. 2009. Infants use shared experience to interpret pointing gestures. *Developmental Science* 12. 264–271. https://doi.org/10.1111/j.1467-7687.2008.00758.x.

Lister, Casey J., Tiarn Burtenshaw, Bradley Walker, Jeneva L. Ohan & Nicolas Fay. 2021. A cross-sectional test of sign creation by children in the gesture and vocal modalities. *Child Development* 92(6). 2395–2412. https://doi.org/10.1111/cdev.13587.

Lister, Casey J., Bradley Walker & Nicolas Fay. 2020. Innovation and enculturation in child communication: A cross-sectional study. *Evolutionary Human Sciences* 2. e56. https://doi.org/10.1017/ehs.2020.57.

Liszkowski, Ulf, Malinda Carpenter, Anne Henning, Tricia Striano & Michael Tomasello. 2004. Twelve-month-olds point to share attention and interest. *Developmental Science* 7. 297–307. https://doi.org/10.1111/j.1467-7687.2004.00349.x.

Little, Hannah, Heikki Rasilo, Sabine van der Ham & Kerem Eryılmaz. 2017. Empirical approaches for investigating the origins of structure in speech. *Interaction Studies: Social Behaviour and Communication in Biological and Artificial Systems* 18(3). 330–351. https://doi.org/10.1075/is.18.3.03lit.

Lombao, Diego, Miquel Guardiola & Marina Mosquera. (2017). Teaching to make stone tools: New experimental evidence supporting a technological hypothesis for the origins of language. *Scientific Reports* 7(1). 14394. https://doi.org/10.1038/s41598-017-14322-y.

Lucy, John A. 2016. Recent advances in the study of linguistic relativity in historical context: A critical assessment. *Language Learning* 66(3). 487–515. https://doi.org/10.1111/lang.12195.

Lyn, Heidi. 2012. Apes and the evolution of language: Taking stock of 40 years of research. In Todd K. Shackelford & Jennifer Vonk (eds.), *The Oxford handbook of comparative evolutionary psychology*, 356–378. Oxford: Oxford University Press.

Lyn, Heidi, Jamie L. Russell, David A. Leavens et al. 2014. Apes communicate about absent and displaced objects: Methodology matters. *Animal Cognition* 17(1).85–94. https://doi.org/10.1007/s10071-013-0640-0.

Macedonia, Joseph M. & Christopher S. Evans. 1993. Essay on contemporary issues in ethology: Variation among mammalian alarm call systems and the problem of meaning in animal signals. *Ethology* 93(3). 177–197. https://doi.org/10.1111/j.1439-0310.1993.tb00988.x.

Maclarnon, Ann. 2012. The anatomical and physiological basis of human speech production: Adaptations and exaptations. In Maggie Tallerman & Kathleen R. Gibson (eds.), *The Oxford handbook of language evolution*, 224–235. Oxford: Oxford University Press.

Macuch Silva, Vinicius, Judith Holler, Asli Ozyurek & Seán G. Roberts. 2020. Multimodality and the origin of a novel communication system in face-to-face interaction. *Royal Society Open Science* 7(1). 182056. https://doi.org/10.1098/rsos.182056.

Matthews, Danielle, Elena Lieven & Michael Tomasello. 2010. What's in a manner of speaking? Children's sensitivity to partner-specific referential precedents. *Developmental Psychology* 46. 749–760. https://doi.org/10.1037/a0019657.

McBrearty, Sally & Alison S. Brooks. 2000. The revolution that wasn't: A new interpretation of the origin of modern human behavior. *Journal of Human Evolution* 39(5). 453–563. https://doi.org/10.1006/jhev.2000.0435.

Mcburney, Susan Lloyd. 2001. William Stokoe and the discipline of sign language linguistics. *Historiographia Linguistica* 28(1–2). 143–186. https://doi.org/10.1075/hl.28.1.10mcb.

McMahon, April. S. 1994. *Understanding language change*. Cambridge: Cambridge University Press.

Meir, Irit, Wendy Sandler, Carol Padden & Mark Aronoff. 2010. Emerging sign languages. In Marc Marschark & Patricia Elizabeth Spencer (eds.), *The Oxford handbook of deaf studies, language, and education*, Vol. 2, 267–280. Oxford University Press.

Meltzoff, Andrew N. & Rechele Brooks. 2008. Self-experience as a mechanism for learning about others: A training study in social cognition. *Developmental Psychology* 44(5). 1257–1265. https://doi.org/10.1037/a0012888.

Mendívil-Giró, José-Luis. 2019. Did language evolve through language change? On language change, language evolution and grammaticalization theory. *Glossa* 4(1). 124. https://doi.org/10.5334/gjgl.895.

Meneganzin, Andra & Adrian Currie. 2022. Behavioural modernity, investigative disintegration & Rubicon expectation. *Synthese* 200(1). 47. https://doi.org/10.1007/s11229-022-03491-7.

Meneganzin, Andra, Telmo Pievani & Giorgio Manzi. 2022. Pan-Africanism vs. single-origin of Homo sapiens: Putting the debate in the light of evolutionary biology. *Evolutionary Anthropology* 31(4). 199–212. https://doi.org/10.1002/evan.21955.

Menzel, Randolf. 2012. The honeybee as a model for understanding the basis of cognition. *Nature Reviews Neuroscience* 13(11). 758–768. https://doi.org/10.1038/nrn3357.

Miles, H. Lyn. 1999. Symbolic communication with and by great apes. In Sue Taylor Parker, Robert W. Mitchell & H. Lyn Miles (eds.), *The mentalities of gorillas and orangutans: Comparative perspectives*, 197–210. Cambridge: Cambridge University Press.

Mineiro, Ana, Inmaculada Concepción Báez-Montero, Mara Moita, Isabel Galhano-Rodrigues & Alexandre Castro-Caldas. 2021. Disentangling pantomime from early sign in a new sign language: Window into language evolution research. *Frontiers in Psychology* 12. www.frontiersin.org/articles/10.3389/fpsyg.2021.640057. (23 May 2023).

Mineiro, Ana, Patrícia Carmo, Cristina Caroça et al. 2017. Emerging linguistic features of Sao Tome and Principe sign language. *Sign Language & Linguistics*. John Benjamins 20(1). 109–128. https://doi.org/10.1075/sll.20.1.04min.

Moll, Henrike, Malinda Carpenter & Michael Tomasello. 2007. Fourteen-month-olds know what others experience only in joint engagement with them. *Developmental Science* 10. 826–835. https://doi.org/10.1111/j.1467-7687.2007.00615.x.

Moore, Richard. 2014. Ape gestures: Interpreting chimpanzee and bonobo minds. *Current Biology* 24(14). R645–R647. https://doi.org/10.1016/j.cub.2014.05.072.

Moore, Richard. 2017. Social cognition, stag hunts, and the evolution of language. *Biology & Philosophy* 32(6). 797–818. https://doi.org/10.1007/s10539-017-9598-7.

Morin, Olivier, James Winters, Thomas F. Müller et al. 2018. What smartphone apps may contribute to language evolution research. *Journal of Language Evolution* 3(2). 91–93. https://doi.org/10.1093/jole/lzy005.

Morin, Olivier, Thomas F. Müller, Tiffany Morisseau & James Winters. 2022. Cultural evolution of precise and agreed-upon semantic conventions in a multiplayer gaming app. *Cognitive Science* 46(2). e13113. https://doi.org/10.1111/cogs.13113.

Morgan, Thomas J. H., Natalie T. Uomini, Luke E. Rendell et al. 2015. Experimental evidence for the co-evolution of hominin tool-making teaching and language. *Nature Communications* 6(1). 6029. https://doi.org/10.1038/ncomms7029.

Motamedi, Yasamin, Kenny Smith, Marieke Schouwstra, Jennifer Culbertson & Simon Kirby. 2021. The emergence of systematic argument distinctions in artificial sign languages. *Journal of Language Evolution* 6(2). 77–98. https://doi.org/10.1093/jole/lzab002.

Neisser, Arden. 1983. *The other side of silence: Sign language and the deaf community in America*. Washington, DC: Gallaudet University Press.

Newman, James L. 2013. *Encountering gorillas: A chronicle of discovery, exploitation, understanding, and survival*. Lanham: Rowman & Littlefield.

Newson, Lesley & Peter Richerson. 2021. *A story of us: A new look at human evolution*. Oxford: Oxford University Press.

Nölle, Jonas & Bruno Galantucci. 2022. Experimental semiotics. In Adolfo M. García & Agustín Ibáñez (eds.), *The Routledge handbook of semiosis and the brain*, 66–81. New York: Routledge.

Nölle, Jonas, Riccardo Fusaroli, Gregory J. Mills & Kristian Tylén. 2020a. Language as shaped by the environment: Linguistic construal in a collaborative spatial task. *Palgrave Communications* 6(1). 27. https://doi.org/10.1057/s41599-020-0404-9.

Nölle, Jonas, Simon Kirby & Kenny Smith. 2020b. Does environment shape spatial language? A virtual reality experiment. In Andrea Ravignani, Chiara Barbieri, Mauricio Martins et al. (eds.), *The evolution of language: Proceedings of the 13th International Conference* (EvoLang13), 321–323. https://doi.org/10.17617/2.3190925.

Nölle, Jonas, Marlene Staib, Riccardo Fusaroli & Kristian Tylén. 2018. The emergence of systematicity: How environmental and communicative factors shape a novel communication system. *Cognition* 181. 93–104. https://doi.org/10.1016/j.cognition.2018.08.014.

Odling-Smee, John & Laland, Kevin N. 2009. Cultural niche-construction: evolution's cradle of language. In Rudolf Botha & Chris Knight (eds.), *The Prehistory of Language*, 99–112. Oxford: Oxford University Press.

O'Grady, William, John Archibald, Mark Aronoff & Janie Rees-Miller (eds.). 2017. *Contemporary linguistics: An introduction*. Boston: Bedford/St. Martin's.

Oller, D. Kimbrough. 2004. Underpinnings for a theory of communicative evolution. In D. Kimbrough Oller & Ulrike Griebel (eds.), *Evolution of communication systems: A comparative approach*, 49–65. Cambridge, MA: MIT Press.

Oller, D. Kimbrough & Ulrike Griebel (eds.). 2004. *Evolution of communication systems: A comparative approach*. Cambridge, MA: MIT Press.

Owren, Michael J., Jacquelyn A. Dieter, Robert M. Seyfarth & Dorothy L. Cheney. 1993. Vocalizations of rhesus (Macaca mulatta) and Japanese (M. Fuscata) macaques cross-fostered between species show evidence of only limited modification. *Developmental Psychobiology: The Journal of the International Society for Developmental Psychobiology*. Wiley Online Library 26(7). 389–406.

Pack, Adam A. 2015. Experimental studies of dolphin cognitive abilities. In Denise L. Herzing & Christine M. Johnson (eds.), *Dolphin communication and cognition: Past, present, and future*, 175–200. Cambridge, MA: MIT Press.

Pepperberg, Irene M. 2012. Symbolic communication in the grey Parrot. In Todd K. Shackelford & Jennifer Vonk (eds.), *The Oxford handbook of comparative evolutionary psychology*, 297–319. Oxford: Oxford University Press.

Perniss, Pamela, Robin Thompson & Gabriella Vigliocco. 2010. Iconicity as a general property of language: Evidence from spoken and signed languages. *Frontiers in Psychology* 1. 227. https://doi.org/10.3389/fpsyg.2010.00227.

Parravicini, Andrea & Telmo Pievani. 2019. Mosaic evolution in hominin phylogeny: Meanings, implications, and explanations. *Journal of Anthropological Sciences* 97. 45–68. https://doi.org/10.4436/jass.97001.

Petkov, Christopher I. & Carel ten Cate. 2020. Structured sequence learning: Animal abilities, cognitive operations, and language evolution. *Topics in Cognitive Science* 12(3). 828–842.

Petré, Peter & Lynn Anthonissen. 2020. Individuality in complex systems: A constructionist approach. Cognitive Linguistics 31(2). 185–212. https://doi.org/10.1515/cog-2019-0033.

Petré, Peter & Freek Van de Velde. 2018. The real-time dynamics of the individual and the community in grammaticalization. Language 94(4). 867–901.

Pijpops, Dirk. 2020. What is an alternation? Six answers. *Belgian Journal of Linguistics* 34. 283–294. https://doi.org/10.1075/bjl.00052.pij.

Pilley, John W. & Alliston K. Reid. 2011. Border collie comprehends object names as verbal referents. *Behavioural Processes* 86(2). 184–195. https://doi.org/10.1016/j.beproc.2010.11.007.

Planer, Ronald & Kim Sterelny. 2021. *From signal to symbol: The evolution of language.* Cambridge, MA: MIT Press.

Pleyer, Michael. 2017. Protolanguage and mechanisms of meaning construal in interaction. *Language Sciences* 63. 69–90. https://doi.org/10.1016/j.langsci.2017.01.003.

Pleyer, Michael. 2020. *The everyday use of pretend in child language and child-directed speech: A corpus study.* Heidelberg: heiDOK. https://doi.org/10.11588/heidok.00028873.

Pleyer, Michael. 2023. The role of interactional and cognitive mechanisms in the evolution of (proto)language(s). *Lingua* 282. 103458. https://doi.org/10.1016/j.lingua.2022.103458.

Pleyer, Michael & Stefan Hartmann. 2020. Construction grammar for monkeys?: Animal communication and its implications for language evolution in the light of usage-based linguistic theory. *Evolutionary Linguistic Theory* 2(2). 154–196. https://doi.org/10.1075/elt.00021.ple.

Pleyer, Michael, Stefan Hartmann, James Winters & Jordan Zlatev. 2017. Interaction and iconicity in the evolution of language: Introduction to the special issue. *Interaction Studies* 18(3). 303–313. https://doi.org/10.1075/is.18.3.01ple.

Pleyer, Michael, Ryan Lepic & Stefan Hartmann. 2022. Compositionality in different modalities: A view from usage-based linguistics. *International Journal of Primatology.* https://doi.org/10.1007/s10764-022-00330-x.

Pleyer, Michael, Svetlana Kuleshova & Elizabeth Qing Zhang. 2023. Analogy and the evolution of the cognitive foundations of metaphor: A comparative and archaeological perspective. In M. Goldwater, F. K. Anggoro, B. K. Hayes & D. C. Ong (eds.), *Proceedings of the 45th Annual Conference of the Cognitive Science Society.* 2541–2549. https://escholarship.org/uc/item/2g59r2k8.

Pleyer, Michael & James Winters. 2014. Integrating cognitive linguistics and language evolution research. *Theoria et Historia Scientiarum* 11. 19–43. https://doi.org/10.12775/ths-2014-002.

Pleyer, Michael & Elizabeth Qing Zhang. 2022. Re-evaluating Hockett's design features from a cognitive and neuroscience perspective: The case of displacement. In A. Ravignani, R. Asano, D. Valente, et al. (eds.), *Proceedings of the Joint Conference on Language Evolution (JCoLE).* 586–589. https://doi.org/10.17617/2.3398549.

Pleyer, Monika & Michael Pleyer. 2016. The evolution of im/politeness. In S. G. Roberts, C. Cuskley, L. McCrohon, et al. (eds.), *The evolution of language: Proceedings of the 11th International Conference on the Evolution of Language (EVOLANG 11)*. New Orleans. http://evolang.org/neworleans/papers/176.html.

Pleyer, Monika & Michael Pleyer. 2022. An evolutionary perspective on im/politeness and the pragmatic concept of face. In A. Ravignani, R. Asano, D. Valente, et al. (eds.), *Proceedings of the Joint Conference on Language Evolution (JCoLE)*. 590–597. https://doi.org/10.17617/2.3398549.

Ponce de León, Marcia S., Thibault Bienvenu, Assaf Marom et al. 2021. The primitive brain of early *Homo*. *Science 372*(6538), 165–171. https://doi.org/10.1126/science.aaz0032.

Potts, Richard. 2013. Hominin evolution in settings of strong environmental variability. *Quaternary Science Reviews* 73. 1–13. https://doi.org/10.1016/j.quascirev.2013.04.003.

Pouw, Wim & Susanne Fuchs. 2022. Origins of vocal-entangled gesture. *Neuroscience & Biobehavioral Reviews* 141. 104836. https://doi.org/10.1016/j.neubiorev.2022.104836.

Premack, David 1971. Language in chimpanzee? *Science (New York, N.Y.)* 172(3985). 808–822. https://doi.org/10.1126/science.172.3985.808.

Premack, David & Guy Woodruff. 1978. Does the chimpanzee have a theory of mind? *Behavioral and Brain Sciences* 1. 515–526.

Price, Tabitha, Philip Wadewitz, Dorothy Cheney et al. 2015. Vervets revisited: A quantitative analysis of alarm call structure and context specificity. *Scientific Reports* 5(1). 1–11. https://doi.org/10.1038/srep13220.

Radden, Günther & René Dirven. 2007. *Cognitive English grammar*. Amsterdam: John Benjamins.

Radick, Gregory. 2007. *The simian tongue: The long debate about animal language*. Chicago: University of Chicago Press.

Raviv, Limor, Antje Meyer & Shiri Lev-Ari. 2019. Compositional structure can emerge without generational transmission. *Cognition* 182. 151–164. https://doi.org/10.1016/j.cognition.2018.09.010.

Raviv, Limor & Inbal Arnon. 2018. Systematicity, but not compositionality: Examining the emergence of linguistic structure in children and adults using iterated learning. *Cognition* 181. 160–173. https://doi.org/10.1016/j.cognition.2018.08.011,

Riebel, Katharina, Karan J. Odom, Naomi E. Langmore & Michelle L. Hall. 2019. New insights from female bird song: Towards an integrated approach to studying male and female communication roles. *Biology Letters* 15(4). 20190059. https://doi.org/10.1098/rsbl.2019.0059.

Ritt, Nikolaus. 2004. *Selfish sounds and linguistic evolution: A Darwinian approach to language change*. Cambridge: Cambridge University Press.

Roberts, Gareth. 2017. The linguist's Drosophila: Experiments in language change. *Linguistics Vanguard* 3(1). 20160086. https://doi.org/10.1515/ling van-2016-0086.

Roberts, Seán G. 2018. Robust, causal, and incremental approaches to investigating linguistic adaptation. *Frontiers in Psychology 9*. https://doi.org/10.3389/fpsyg.2018.00166.

Roberts, Seán G., Anton Killin, Angarika Deb et al. 2020. CHIELD: The causal hypotheses in evolutionary linguistics database. *Journal of Language Evolution* 5(2). 101–120. https://doi.org/10.1093/jole/lzaa001.

Rosch, Eleanor. 1978. Principles of categorization. In Eleanor Rosch & Barbara B. Lloyd (eds.), *Cognition and categorization*, 27–48. Hillsdale, NJ: Erlbaum.

Rubio-Fernandez, Paula. 2023. Cultural evolutionary pragmatics: Investigating the codevelopment and coevolution of language and social cognition. *Psychological Review*. https://doi.org/10.1037/rev0000423

Rumbaugh, Duane M. 1977. *Language learning by a chimpanzee: The Lana project*. New York: Academic Press.

Savage-Rumbaugh, E. Sue, Jeannine Murphy, Rose A. Sevcik et al. 1993. Language comprehension in ape and child. *Monographs of the Society for Research in Child Development* 58(3–4). 1–222.

Savage-Rumbaugh, E. Sue, James L. Pate, Janet Lawson, S. Tom Smith & Steven Rosenbaum. 1983. Can a chimpanzee make a statement? *Journal of Experimental Psychology: General* 112. 457–492. https://doi.org/10.1037/0096-3445.112.4.457.

Scarantino, Andrea & Zanna Clay. 2015. Contextually variable signals can be functionally referential. *Animal Behaviour* (100). e1–e8. https://doi.org/10.1016/j.anbehav.2014.08.017.

Scerri, Eleanor M. L. & Manuel Will. 2023. The revolution that still isn't: The origins of behavioral complexity in Homo sapiens. *Journal of Human Evolution* 179.103358. https://doi.org/10.1016/j.jhevol.2023.103358.

Schleicher, August. 1863. *Die Darwinische Theorie und die Sprachwissenschaft: Offenes Sendschreiben an Herrn Dr. Ernst Haeckel, o. Professor der Zoologie und Direktor des zoologischen Museums an der Universität Jena*. 2nd ed. Weimar: Böhlau.

Schlenker, Philippe, Emmanuel Chemla, Kate Arnold et al. 2014. Monkey semantics: Two 'Dialects' of Campbell's monkey alarm calls. *Linguistics and Philosophy* 37(6). 439–501. https://doi.org/10.1007/s10988-014-9155-7.

Schlenker, Philippe, Emmanuel Chemla, Anne M. Schel et al. 2016. Formal monkey linguistics. *Theoretical Linguistics* 42(1–2). 1–90. https://doi.org/10.1515/tl-2016-0001.

Schmid, Hans-Jörg (ed.). 2016. *Entrenchment and the psychology of language learning: How we reorganize and adapt linguistic knowledge* (Language and the Human Lifespan). Berlin: De Gruyter.

Schmid, Hans-Jörg. 2020. *The dynamics of the linguistic system: Usage, conventionalization, and entrenchment.* Oxford: Oxford University Press.

Searcy, William A. & Malte Andersson. 1986. Sexual selection and the evolution of song. *Annual Review of Ecology and Systematics* 17(1). 507–533. https://doi.org/10.1146/annurev.es.17.110186.002451.

Sebeok, Thomas A. & Jean Umiker-Sebeok. 1980. *Speaking of apes: A critical anthology of two-way communication with man.* New York: Plenum.

Seed, Amanda & Michael Tomasello. 2010. Primate cognition. *Topics in Cognitive Science* 2. 407–419. https://doi.org/10.1111/j.1756-8765.2010.01099.x.

Seidenberg, Mark S. & Laura A. Petitto. 1979. Signing behavior in apes: A critical review. *Cognition* 7(2). 177–215. https://doi.org/10.1016/0010-0277(79)90019-2.

Selten, Richard & Massimo Warglien. 2007. The emergence of simple languages in an experimental coordination game. *Proceedings of the National Academy of Sciences* 104(18). 7361–7366. https://doi.org/10.1073/pnas.0702077104.

Senghas, Ann, Sotaro Kita & Asli Özyürek. 2004. Children creating core properties of language: Evidence from an emerging sign language in Nicaragua. *Science* 305(5691). 1779–1782. https://doi.org/10.1126/science.1100199.

Senju, Atsushi, Victoria Southgate, Charlotte Snape, Mark Leonard & Gergely Csibra. 2011. Do 18-month-olds really attribute mental states to others? A critical test. *Psychological Science* 22(7). 878–880. https://doi.org/10.1177%2F0956797611411584.

Seyfarth, Robert M. & Dorothy L. Cheney. 1986. Vocal development in vervet monkeys. *Animal Behaviour* 34(6). 1640–1658. https://doi.org/10.1016/S0003-3472(86)80252-4.

Seyfarth, Robert M. & Dorothy L. Cheney. 2010. Production, usage, and comprehension in animal vocalizations. *Brain and Language* 115(1). 92–100. https://doi.org/10.1016/j.bandl.2009.10.003.

Seyfarth, Robert M. & Dorothy L. Cheney. 2015. Social cognition. *Animal Behaviour* 103. 191–202. https://doi.org/10.1016/j.anbehav.2015.01.030.

Sherkina-Lieber, Marina. 2020. A classification of receptive bilinguals: Why we need to distinguish them, and what they have in common. *Linguistic Approaches to Bilingualism* 10(3), 412–440. https://doi.org/10.1075/lab.17080.she.

Sherwood, Chet C. 2019. Human brain evolution. In Todd Shackelford & Viviana Weekes-Shackelford (eds.), *Encyclopedia of evolutionary psychological science*. Cham: Springer. https://doi.org/10.1007/978-3-319-16999-6_813-1

Shilton, Dor. 2019. Is language necessary for the social transmission of lithic technology? *Journal of Language Evolution* 4(2). 124–133. https://doi.org/10.1093/jole/lzz004.

Silvey, Catriona, Simon Kirby & Kenny Smith. 2015. Word meanings evolve to selectively preserve distinctions on salient dimensions. *Cognitive Science* 39(1). 212–226. https://doi.org/10.1111/cogs.12150.

Sinha, Chris. 2015. Language and other artifacts: Socio-cultural dynamics of niche construction. *Frontiers in Psychology* 6. 1601. https://doi.org/10.3389/fpsyg.2015.01601.

Sinha, Chris. 2017. *Ten lectures on language, culture and mind: Cultural, developmental, and evolutionary perspectives in cognitive linguistics* (Distinguished Lectures in Cognitive Linguistics 6). Boston: Brill.

Slobin, Dan I. 1996. From 'thought and language' to 'thinking for speaking'. In John J. Gumperz & Stephen C. Levinson (eds.), *Rethinking linguistic relativity*, 70–96. Cambridge: Cambridge University Press.

Smith, John Maynard & David Harper. 2003. *Animal signals*. Oxford: Oxford University Press.

Sperber, Dan & Deirdre Wilson. 1995. *Relevance: Communication and cognition*. Malden, MA: Blackwell.

Steels, Luc. 2011. Modeling the cultural evolution of language. *Physics of Life Reviews* 8. 339–356. https://doi.org/10.1016/j.plrev.2011.10.014.

Steels, Luc & Tony Belpaeme. 2005. Coordinating perceptually grounded categories through language: A case study for colour. *Behavioral and Brain Sciences* 28(4). 469–488. https://doi.org/10.1017/s0140525x05000087.

Stegmann, Ulrich E. (ed.). 2013. *Animal communication theory: Information and influence*. Cambridge: Cambridge University Press.

Stephan, Claudia & Klaus Zuberbühler. 2016. Persistent females and compliant males coordinate alarm calling in Diana Monkeys. *Current Biology* 26(21). 2907–2912. https://doi.org/10.1016/j.cub.2016.08.033.

Sterelny, Kim. (2012). *The evolved apprentice: How evolution made humans unique*. Cambridge, MA: MIT Press.

Stokoe, William C. 1978. Sign language versus spoken language. *Sign Language Studies* 18(1). 69–90.

Stokoe, William C., Jr. 2005. Sign language structure: An outline of the visual communication systems of the American deaf. *The Journal of Deaf Studies and Deaf Education* 10(1). 3–37. https://doi.org/10.1093/deafed/eni001.

Suddendorf, Thomas. 2008. Explaining human cognitive autapomorphies. *Behavioral and Brain Sciences* 31(2). 147–148. https://doi.org/10.1017/S0140525X08003737.

Suddendorf, Thomas & Michael C. Corballis. 2007. The evolution of foresight: What is mental time travel, and is it unique to humans? *Behavioral and Brain Sciences* 30(3). 299–313. https://doi.org/10.1017/S0140525X07001975.

Suzuki, Toshitaka N. 2018. Alarm calls evoke a visual search image of a predator in birds. *Proceedings of the National Academy of Sciences* 115(7). 1541–1545. https://doi.org/10.1073/pnas.1718884115.

Suzuki, Toshitaka N., David Wheatcroft & Michael Griesser. 2016. Experimental evidence for compositional syntax in bird calls. *Nature Communications* 7(1). 10986. https://doi.org/10.1038/ncomms10986.

Szczepaniak, Renata. 2011. *Grammatikalisierung im Deutschen: Eine Einführung*. 2nd ed. Tübingen: Narr.

Tallerman, Maggie. 2012. Protolanguage. In Maggie Tallerman & Kathleen R. Gibson (eds.), *The Oxford handbook of language evolution*, 479–491. Oxford: Oxford University Press.

Tamariz, Mónica. 2014. Experiments and simulations can inform evolutionary theories of the cultural evolution of language. In Marco Pina & Nathalie Gontier (eds.), *The Evolution of Social Communication in Primates*, vol. 1, 249–288. Cham: Springer.

Tamariz, Monica. 2017. Experimental studies on the cultural evolution of language. *Annual Review of Linguistics* 3(1). 389–407. https://doi.org/10.1146/annurev-linguistics-011516-033807.

Tamariz, Monica & Simon Kirby. 2016. The cultural evolution of language. *Current Opinion in Psychology* 8. 37–43. https://doi.org/10.1016/j.copsyc.2015.09.003.

Taylor, John R. 2003. *Linguistic categorization*. 3rd ed. Oxford: Oxford University Press.

Templin, Mildred C. 1957. *Certain language skills in children: Their development and interrelationships*. Minneapolis: University of Minnesota Press.

ten Cate, Carel. 2017. Assessing the uniqueness of language: Animal grammatical abilities take center stage. *Psychonomic Bulletin & Review* 24(1). 91–96. https://doi.org/10.3758/s13423-016-1091-9.

ten Cate, Carel & Christopher I. Petkov. 2019. The grammatical abilities of animals: A comparative overview. In Peter Hagoort (ed.), *Human language: From genes and brains to behavior*, 687–700. Cambridge, MA: MIT Press.

Terrace, Herbert S., Laura Ann Petitto, Richard Jay Sanders & Thomas G. Bever. 1979. Can an ape create a sentence? *Science* 206(4421). 891–902. https://doi.org/10.1126/science.504995.

Tinits, Peeter, Jonas Nölle & Stefan Hartmann. 2017. Usage context influences the evolution of overspecification in iterated learning. *Journal of Language Evolution* 2(2). 148–159. https://doi.org/10.1093/jole/lzx011.

Tomasello, Michael. 1999. *The cultural origins of human cognition*. Cambridge, MA: Harvard University Press.

Tomasello, Michael. 2003. *Constructing a language: A usage-based theory of language acquisition*. Harvard: Harvard University Press.

Tomasello, Michael. 2008. *Origins of human communication*. Cambridge, MA: MIT Press.

Tomasello, Michael. 2014. *A natural history of human thinking*. Cambridge, MA: Harvard University Press.

Tomasello, Michael. 2017. What did we learn from the ape language studies? In Brian Hare & Shinya Yamamoto (eds.), *Bonobos: Unique in mind, brain, and behavior*, 95–104. Oxford University Press.

Tomasello, Michael & Michelle E. Barton. 1994. Learning words in non-ostensive contexts. *Developmental Psychology* 30. 639–650. https://psycnet.apa.org/doi/10.1037/0012-1649.30.5.639.

Tomasello, Michael, Malinda Carpenter, Josep Call, Tanya Behne & Henrike Moll. 2005. Understanding and sharing intentions: The origins of cultural cognition. *Behavioral and Brain Sciences* 28(5). 675–691. https://doi.org/10.1017/s0140525x05000129.

Tomasello, Michael & Melinda Carpenter. 2007. Shared intentionality. *Developmental Science* 10(1). 121–125. https://doi.org/10.1111/j.1467-7687.2007.00573.x.

Tomasello, Michael & Katherina Haberl. 2003. Understanding attention: 12- and 18-month-olds know what's new for other persons. *Developmental Psychology* 39. 906–912. https://psycnet.apa.org/doi/10.1037/0012-1649.39.5.906.

Townsend, Simon W. & Marta B. Manser. 2013. Functionally referential communication in mammals: The past, present and the future. *Ethology* 119(1). 1–11. https://doi.org/10.1111/eth.12015.

Townsend, Simon W., Sabrina Engesser, Sabine Stoll, Klaus Zuberbühler & Balthasar Bickel. 2018. Compositionality in animals and humans. *PLoS Biology* 16(8). E2006425. https://doi.org/10.1371/journal.pbio.2006425

Townsend, Simon W., Sonja E. Koski, Richard W. Byrne, et al. 2017. Exorcising Grice's ghost: An empirical approach to studying intentional communication in animals. *Biological Reviews* 92(3). 1427–1433. https://doi.org/10.1111/brv.12289.

Truswell, Robert. 2017. Dendrophobia in bonobo comprehension of spoken English. *Mind & Language* 32(4). 395–415. https://doi.org/10.1111/mila.12150.

Tulving, Endel. 2001. Episodic memory and common sense: How far apart? *Philosophical Transactions of the Royal Society of London. Series B: Biological Sciences* 356(1413). 1505–1515. https://doi.org/10.1098/rstb.2001.0937.

Ungerer, Tobias & Stefan Hartmann. 2020. Delineating extravagance: Assessing speakers' perceptions of imaginative constructional patterns. *Belgian Journal of Linguistics* 34. 345–356. https://doi.org/10.1075/bjl.00058.ung.

Ungerer, Tobias & Stefan Hartmann. 2023. *Constructionist approaches: Past, present, future.* Cambridge: Cambridge University Press.

Uryu, Michiko, Sune V. Steffensen & Claire Kramsch. 2014. The ecology of intercultural interaction: Timescales, temporal ranges and identity dynamics. *Language Sciences* 41. 41–59. https://doi.org/10.1016/j.langsci.2013.08.006.

Van de Velde, Freek. 2014. Degeneracy: The maintenance of constructional networks. In Ronny Boogaart, Timothy Colleman & Gijsbert Rutten (eds.), *Extending the scope of construction grammar*, 141–180. Berlin: De Gruyter.

Ventura, Rafael, Joshua B. Plotkin & Gareth Roberts. 2022. Drift as a driver of language change: An artificial language experiment. *Cognitive Science* 46(9). e13197. https://doi.org/10.1111/cogs.13197.

Verendeev, Andrew & Chet C. Sherwood. 2018. Human brain evolution. *Current Opinion in Behavioral Sciences* 16, 41–45. https://doi.org/10.1016/j.cobeha.2017.02.003.

Verhagen, Arie. forthcoming. Evolution in linguistics – innovation, metonymy, and miscommunication. *Cognitive Semantics*.

Verhagen, Arie. 2007. Construal and perspectivization. In Dirk Geeraerts & Herbert Cuyckens (eds.), *The Oxford Handbook of cognitive linguistics*, 48–81. Oxford: Oxford University Press.

Verhagen, Arie. 2021. *Ten lectures on cognitive evolutionary linguistics* (Distinguished Lectures in Cognitive Linguistics 24). Leiden: Brill.

Verhoef, Tessa. 2012. The origins of duality of patterning in artificial whistled languages. *Language and Cognition* 4(4). 357–380. https://doi.org/10.1515/langcog-2012-0019.

Verhoef, Tessa, Simon Kirby & Bart de Boer. 2016. Iconicity and the emergence of combinatorial structure in language. *Cognitive Science* 40(8). 1969–1994. https://doi.org/10.1111/cogs.12326.

Vonk, Jennifer. 2020. Forty years on from the question of referential signals in nonhuman communication. *Animal Behavior and Cognition* 7(2). 82–86. https://doi.org/10.26451/abc.07.02.01.2020

Wacewicz, Sławomir & Przemysław Żywiczyński. 2015. Language evolution: Why Hockett's design features are a non-starter. *Biosemiotics* 8(1). 29–46. https://doi.org/10.1007/s12304-014-9203-2.

Wacewicz, Sławomir & Przemysław Żywiczyński. 2017. The multimodal origins of linguistic communication. *Language & Communication* 54. 1–8. https://doi.org/10.1016/j.langcom.2016.10.001.

Wacewicz, Sławomir & Przymesław Żywiczyński. 2018. Language origins: Fitness consequences, platform of trust, cooperation, and turn-taking. *Interaction Studies* 19(1–2). 167–182. https://doi.org/10.1075/is.17031.wac.

Wacewicz, Sławomir, Przemyslaw Zywiczynski, Stefan Hartmann, Michael Pleyer & Antonio Benítez-Burraco. 2020. 'Language' in language evolution research: Towards a pluralistic view. *Biolinguistics* 14. 59–101. https://doi.org/10.5964/bioling.v14.si.

Wacewicz, Sławomir, Michael Pleyer, Aleksandra Szczepańska, Aleksandra Ewa Poniewierska & Przemysław Żywiczyński. 2023a. The representation of animal communication and language evolution in introductory linguistics textbooks. *Journal of Language Evolution*. https://doi.org/10.1093/jole/lzac010.

Wacewicz, Sławomir, Marta Sibierska, Marek Placinski et al. 2023b. The scientometric landscape of Evolang: A comprehensive database of the Evolang conference. *Journal of Language Evolution* 8(*1*). 102–114. https://doi.org/10.1093/jole/lzad003

Watson, Stuart K., Piera Filippi, Luca Gasparri et al. 2022. Optionality in animal communication: A novel framework for examining the evolution of arbitrariness. *Biological Reviews* 97(6). 2057–2075. https://doi.org/10.1111/brv.12882.

Wheeler, Brandon C. & Julia Fischer. 2012. Functionally referential signals: A promising paradigm whose time has passed. *Evolutionary Anthropology* 21(5). 195–205. https://doi.org/10.1002/evan.21319.

Whiten, Andrew. 2019. Cultural evolution in animals. *Annual Review of Ecology, Evolution, and Systematics* 50(1). 27–48. https://doi.org/10.1146/annurev-ecolsys-110218-025040.

Wiley, R. Haven. 2018. Design features of language. In Todd K. Shackelford & Viviana A. Weekes-Shackelford (eds.), *Encyclopedia of evolutionary psychological science*, 1–13. Cham: Springer. https://doi.org/10.1007/978-3-319-16999-6_3837-1.

Winters, James, Simon Kirby & Kenny Smith. 2015. Languages adapt to their contextual niche. *Language and Cognition* 7(3). 415–449. https://doi.org/10.1017/langcog.2014.35.

Winters, James, Simon Kirby & Kenny Smith. 2018. Contextual predictability shapes signal autonomy. *Cognition* 176. 15–30. https://doi.org/10.1016/j.cognition.2018.03.002.

Wolfle, Dael L. 1933. The relative stability of first and second syllables in an artificial language. *Language* 9(4). 313. https://doi.org/10.2307/409418.

Zehentner, Eva. 2019. *Competition in language change: The rise of the English dative alternation*. Berlin: De Gruyter.

Zeshan, Ulrike & Connie de Vos (eds.). 2012. *Sign languages in village communities: Anthropological and linguistic insights*. Berlin: De Gruyter.

Zhang, Qing. 2017. *The role of vocal learning in language: Evolution and development*. Barcelona: University of Barcelona dissertation. http://hdl.handle.net/2445/118998.

Zhang, Elizabeth Qing, Edward Ruoyang Shi & Lluís Barceló-Coblijn. 2023a. Categorical perception and language evolution: A comparative and neurological perspective. *Frontiers in Psychology* 14. https://doi.org/10.3389/fpsyg.2023.1110730.

Zhang, Elizabeth Qing, Edward Ruoyang Shi & Michael Pleyer. 2023b. Categorical learning and the cognitive foundations of language evolution and development. In Micah Goldwater, Florencia K. Anggoro, Brett K. Hayes & Desmond C. Ong (eds.), *Proceedings of the 45th Annual Conference of the Cognitive Science Society*. https://escholarship.org/uc/item/4xt399f2.

Zlatev, Jordan, Przemysław Żywiczyński & Sławomir Wacewicz. 2020. Pantomime as the original human-specific communicative system. *Journal of Language Evolution* 5(2). 156–174. https://doi.org/10.1093/jole/lzaa006.

Zuberbühler, K. 2000. Interspecies semantic communication in two forest primates. *Proceedings of the Royal Society B: Biological Sciences* 267 (1444). 713–718. https://doi.org/10.1098/rspb.2000.1061.

Zuberbühler, Klaus. 2002. A syntactic rule in forest monkey communication. *Animal Behaviour* 63(2). 293–299. https://doi.org/10.1006/anbe.2001.1914.

Zuberbühler, Klaus, Dorothy L. Cheney & Robert M. Seyfarth. 1999. Conceptual semantics in a nonhuman primate. *Journal of Comparative Psychology* 113(1). 33–42. https://doi.org/10.1037/0735-7036.113.1.33.

Zuidema, Willem & Bart de Boer. 2018. The evolution of combinatorial structure in language. *Current Opinion in Behavioral Sciences* 21. 138–144. https://doi.org/10.1016/j.cobeha.2018.04.011.

Żywiczyński, Przemysław, Sławomir Wazewicz & Marta Sibierska. 2018. Defining pantomime for language evolution research. *Topoi* 37. 307–318. https://doi.org/10.1007/s11245-016-9425-9.

Acknowledgements

We would like to thank one anonymous and one not-so-anonymous reviewer, as well as Monika Pleyer, for their helpful suggestions and comments.

This research is part of project No. 2021/43/P/HS2/02729 co-funded by the National Science Centre and the European Union Framework Programme for Research and Innovation Horizon 2020 under the Marie Skłodowska-Curie grant agreement No. 945339.

Cambridge Elements ≡

Cognitive Linguistics

About the Series
Cambridge Elements in Cognitive Linguistics aims to extend the theoretical and methodological boundaries of cognitive linguistics. It will advance and develop established areas of research in the discipline, as well as address areas where it has not traditionally been explored and areas where it has yet to become well-established.

Cambridge Elements$^{\equiv}$

Cognitive Linguistics

Elements in the Series

Printed in the USA
CPSIA information can be obtained
at www.ICGtesting.com
CBHW072125270324
5983CB00005B/195